Naima

This edition published in the UK in 2024

Copyright © Naima Chakkour

The right of Naima Chakkour to be identified as the author of this work has been asserted under the Copyright, Designs and Patents Act 1988.

All rights reserved. No part of this publication may be reproduced, stored in a retrieval system, or transmitted in any form or by any means, electronic, mechanical, photocopying, recording or otherwise, without the prior written consent of the publishers.

ISBN: 978-1-3999-9088-2
Photographs © Naima Chakkour

Text and cover design by Agnes Graves

Naima
Undeterred: My MND Story

By Naima Chakkour

Motor neurone disease (MND), also known as amyotrophic lateral sclerosis (ALS), affects the nerves known as motor neurones. These nerves are found in the brain and spinal cord and they help to tell your muscles what to do.

Symptoms include muscle weakness; loss of muscle mass; muscle cramps and spasms (fasciculation); stiff joints; movement and mobility problems; pain and discomfort; speech and communication problems; and breathing problems.

MND cannot be stopped or reversed, but therapies, equipment and medication can help to manage symptoms. MND can significantly shorten life expectancy and, unfortunately, eventually leads to death.

Any profits made from sales of this book will be donated to My Name'5 Doddie Foundation, a charity that works to fund research with a goal of a world free of MND.

www.myname5doddie.co.uk

Contents

Foreword by Felipe González ix

Introduction by Gerald Hattee xiii

Naima: Telling my story 1

Beginnings 5

When things changed 15

This is the reality... 27
    What does it feel like to have MND?

Raising a family 37
    in the shadow of MND

Thirty years with MND 53

Epiphanies 61

Pandemic 77

Now 85

Afterword 103

Acknowledgements 107

Foreword

by Felipe González

(*Friend and former Prime Minister of Spain*)

Dear Naima,

I have spent a lot of time thinking about how to write a foreword for your memoir. What would be a fitting tribute? In the end, I concluded that I could only write you a letter. This is a letter to Naima – to the Naima I have known for so long and whom I respect, admire and love.

It is difficult to explain the feelings I experienced whilst reading your memoir: your account of your life and your emotions through the years of your life. And to read your words as you explain your state of mind at various points in your life. It is hard not to delve into the details and the chapters here. But that would diverge from the purpose of this letter, which is merely to preface the immense and beautiful effort you have made to share your testimony – to offer up a narrative of the life journey of a person like you, affected by ALS/MND.

I met you at Le Mirage, your family's hotel in Tangier. As we talked, I thought about the fact that we inhabited a space above the Caves of Hercules, about which Polybius, the first Greek historian, had written. You appreciated the view of the horizon across the Atlantic Ocean that hugged the coastline all the way down to the town of your childhood. Dear Naima, in these pages you recount your childhood in that small and wonderful town of Asilah, and you take me back to conversations with your brother and the similarities I found with my own family. Being proud of your origins is to honour your parents – the people who imprint on your personality during childhood and early youth and shape you into what you will be throughout your life.

Some speak of heroism when they speak of you. But the truth is, I am greatly impressed by your refusal to have your courage acknowledged. Let us not use grand words. Because being brave does not mean someone does not feel fear. In fact, feeling fear and being able to overcome it is what indicates true bravery and emotional strength. To feel no fear at all cannot be called bravery: it is simply and plainly recklessness. To not feel fear is to be a person who is incapable of having the most basic human emotion. It is entirely natural that in the face of adversity, we feel fear. And nothing can be more adverse than an ALS/MND diagnosis, which limits your life horizon. Only those who finitise themselves, who do not understand the complexities of life, do not feel fear. Those who know fear understand the deepest realities of life. And that is what you unravel in your story when you explain how it all began.

In 1993, you faced an initial diagnosis alone, determined to protect your children and perhaps in denial yourself. By 1996,

Foreword

you came to understand the truth of your situation: a terrible diagnosis you had to accept. I think of the moment when they gave you a life expectancy and you could see the end before you – between three and five years. How could you not be afraid in that moment, dear Naima? It is impossible. But you turned your fear into an emotional strength to overcome it and face the challenges before you. That is what you have done. And that is why we all admire you. You don't like to be called a heroine but you exemplify true bravery, as opposed to recklessness.

The diagnosis came from out of the blue, and you were already both mother and father to all four of your children – including Mehdi who came into your care. All four were your children equally. Because that is one of the most typical and delightful peculiarities of your family: you all embrace each other and the children – they are everyone's children. When your diagnosis became apparent, your whole family rallied around you and I know you are very grateful to your family for the efforts they have made to take care of you, to support you and to seek solutions, even with the knowledge that any solutions were difficult, limited and sometimes felt impossible. However, I don't think you are aware that you have given your family just as much – and possibly even more – than your family has given you.

In a wonderful paradox of existence, as the disease progressed, *you* became the pillar on which everything pivoted. You became the centre of the small community that is your family – your dear brothers, your children and their children – it was all built and developed around you. You might have become the recipient of their love and care but, despite everything, the love and care you returned was just as great. That is you. That is the evidence of your vital courage.

This account of your life brings me closer to you. Your view that death is part of life has always been mine. There are few people one can talk to about these things because, at least in our culture, talking about death is neither common nor acceptable for many people. For me, it is not only acceptable, but entirely natural. Being able to talk openly with you about these things is why I feel so close to you, and now the reflection of you, illustrated through your words in this book, brings me closer to you. And closer to your family who, after many years, is a family that I also feel is mine today.

I love your recollection of asking Adam and Mehdi to bring your wheelchair close to the sea on the beach near Le Mirage. All so you could touch with your feet those waters you freely walked into as a child. Never has laughter and joy been better described as expressions of happiness. And you evoke the unique atmosphere at that place which is where you feel like you are home – the conversations with historians, intellectuals and artists there. It is a space to feel free and extract pieces of happiness from our lives. Le Mirage, in itself, represents something that most reflects the effort of the Chakkour family. And again, you are the pillar on which it stands.

See you soon, Naima. I love you.

Felipe González

Introduction
by Gerald Hattee

I met Naima for the first time twenty years ago. She was due to attend a parents' evening at the school where I was Principal in Kensington, London. She had come to talk about the progress of her son, Mehdi, who was studying for his GCSE exams at the time. I had been told that Naima had MND and I understood what that meant for her. Psychologically, I was prepared to meet someone with a terminal illness and major physical disability – it was not something I had ever experienced before. But Naima was not what I expected. Where I had expected a woman in a wheelchair, she walked – albeit with assistance – through the entrance hall to meet me. The woman I encountered was elegant, warm and vivacious. The radiance

Naima

of her smile was matched by the rigour of her concern for her son Mehdi. I realised, in that brief meeting, that Naima was a woman whose personality and spirit transcended the limits of her condition.

Happily, in the following years, both her daughter Sabrina and her son Adam joined the college as well. From that first meeting, Naima and I began to develop a respect and regard for each other which blossomed – little by little – into the closest and most reliable of friendships. From the beginning, we found we had much in common: an "old fashioned" regard for manners and attention to appearance, and an instinctive rejection of the overly sentimental and self-pitying. We also acknowledged that we had another bond in common: we both had the experience of long-term family illness – Naima's more immediate than my own – and an empathy with others suffering similar difficulties that was based on our own sadness and anxieties around health. In each other we found a kindred spirit.

I was invited to Naima's family home in Tangier, where I was met with the most hospitable of welcomes. I will always remember the kindness of her brothers upon my arrival. It felt very much like home. And so it has been ever since for me and Naima. Now, it is as though we are a part of the same extended family – but a family based on friendship. We have different backgrounds and experiences, and yet we are united through our strong bond of comradeship. I admire Naima's ability to reach out to others, to be imaginative, and the fact that she is always so thoughtful. It helps, of course, that we share a sense of humour. Whilst we are always open with one another about the seriousness and reality of her condition, we are also able to find joy and laughter in our everyday encounters.

Imagination, kindness, warmth, naughtiness, intellect, understanding and helpfulness – these are the qualities of my closest friend, Naima. Extraordinarily – and despite the gradual

Introduction

loss of the use of her limbs and the eroding of her independence – I never think of Naima as disabled. When I think of Naima, I think of a shining light – always ready to give strength and succour to those around her. And now, I am pleased that others can get to know her great spirit through her story.

Naima:
Telling my story

Some years ago, I decided to share the story of my life and my personal experience of the illness that has overtaken me and destroyed my body. As I have lost the physical ability to write as a "normal person" – that is, with a keyboard or a pen – I have had to learn to type another way. My neck and chin have kept some strength and I was advised by Helen, my occupational therapist, to try to use a neck switch to type. It took a few minutes for me to understand the process but I was able to adapt to it fairly quickly. Tapping with a switch on my neck to generate the words to tell my story has taken a lot of time. At times, it has used up my strength and has made my neck ache but, despite the pain, I have carried on writing.

Naima

I persevered because I wanted to share my story about my life and Motor Neurone Disease.

The shocking news of the death of our MND hero, Stephen Hawking the astrophysicist, in 2018 was a matter of great sadness for the world but especially for his fellow MND sufferers. It felt to me as though, when we lost him, we lost a talisman – we had lost a little bit more of our hope. Hawking was diagnosed with MND at the age of twenty-one in 1963. He was given just two years to live at that point. It was perhaps through luck, or maybe through his own fortitude and determination, that Hawking defied those odds and lived with MND for over fifty years. I was given the same news when I received my diagnosis and yet, as I write, I have endured this illness for more than thirty years. My doctor tells me that he only knows of one person who has surpassed that milestone, and that is Hawking.

Hawking's refusal to be cowed by the disease was something I both admired and tried to emulate. When I read that he had aspirations to travel to space, I was both delighted and enthralled by the notion. Some might have seen it as crazy, given his health and the constraints on his physical abilities, but I was absolutely thrilled by the idea that he didn't see this adventure as beyond him. Despite all his suffering, Hawking still wanted to live and have this out-of-this-world experience. He never made the journey to space, but just the fact that he was not frightened to contemplate the idea was so important to me.

People who receive a diagnosis of terminal illness sometimes make a bucket list of things they want to do before they pass away: journeying to a wonderful place, completing a lifelong project or experiencing some longed-for adventure. When I received my diagnosis, my list was very simple because I knew that I wanted just one thing. I had four young children, and I wanted *enough* time with my family so that I could see them grow up safely and be happy. I knew there would come a time when I could no longer care for them the way I had been doing. I wanted, above everything, to be around long enough to see them reach adulthood and know that my job was done. It became my mission in the years after my diagnosis.

I could not have been more blessed because I have had those years I needed to do that. My diagnosis was over thirty years ago and my children are all grown now and they have children of their own. But now, I have come to realise something about that mission that I set myself and that is that I will never truly feel as though I have completed it – no matter how much time I have left. I had set myself the impossible task. I think many parents can relate to this. You never, ever, stop wanting to protect them and to be there for your children. Your child can become a parent themselves – as mine are now – and they will still *always* be your baby.

Writing the story of my life has also helped me to understand that I have had not one but three main inspirations for continuing in my struggle to stay on this earth: not just my love for my children, but the love of my brothers, and my religious faith. I also found another reason for telling my story and that is that I hope it will give strength to others suffering from this terrible disease and inspire the world to support more research into it. Just as I have always taken inspiration from Stephen Hawking's story, I hope, in some modest way, that I too can be someone that others can look to for inspiration. Like him, I have defied the odds and all the medical expectations, just by surviving this long. If I have taken strength from his story over the years, maybe, in telling mine, I can give strength to others facing their own fearful diagnoses.

MND is a rare condition that affects the brain and the nerves. We still have no idea what causes it, and diagnosis can be frustratingly slow. The disease severely reduces life expectancy and most people with a diagnosis die within five years of the onset of symptoms. And it is also perhaps one of the most cruel diseases to affect a person – systematically shutting down parts of the human form until the sufferer is trapped inside their own body. There is still no cure for MND. However, treatments can be used to improve symptoms. There is only one licensed drug in the UK: riluzole. I participated in initial trials when I was invited by Professor Vincent Meininger. The findings showed that the drug had a small effect in slowing the progress of the illness and it was estimated that it might increase survival by two to three months in patients. I have been taking this medication for thirty years.

And so this book has become a part of my mission. It is partly my legacy to my children and my grandchildren, and I hope it will keep the memory of me alive when my time eventually does run out. And I hope that writing about my own experience will help to give courage and hope to fellow sufferers of Motor Neurone Disease. And show that, even in the darkest times, we can realise our seemingly impossible dreams in the face of such adversity.

Beginnings

I was born in Asilah, a small fishing town on the Atlantic coast of Morocco. Originally built by the Portuguese in the seventeenth century, there is a quiet beauty in the town's architecture. There is a small castle, a harbour and narrow streets where houses nestle together. Back then, Asilah was a community built on trust and hard work. The inhabitants lived proudly even on the edge of poverty. And, for me, it was a place of happiness, where the sun shone almost every day. There were very few shadows over my childhood.

I was the youngest of three children in a Muslim family. I had two older brothers, Abdeslam and Ahmed. My father – who lived to over a hundred – owned the first restaurant in Asilah. His generosity to his customers was legendary, though, and he

Naima

eventually had to work as the chef at the local school and college, as he was not making any money from his restaurant business.

My mother was also a good cook. She could make the tastiest of meals out of almost any ingredients that we could afford. Although we were not rich, we enjoyed an incredibly healthy diet, consisting of the cheapest fish, vegetables and fruit – what we ate was always in season – with an occasional treat of meat. In this small town, the main meal for everyone often depended on the day's catch landed by the fishing boats. There were many evenings when everyone dined on the same fish and, on those days, there was the same smell of cooking coming from multiple houses. If the fishermen were lucky, there was the special enjoyment of the more exclusive white fish.

My brothers and I grew up with the sea close by. My father taught me how to swim and, by the age of seven, I was in love with the waves and entirely at home in the water. During the summer, we would almost live on the beach. In the winter, we played in the streets together. Market day on a Thursday was the high point of the week. The neighbouring farmers brought their produce to sell and, in return, they bought fuel, fish and groceries from vendors in the town.

It was a safe world. Nobody locked a front door. I remember that the street lighting was so unreliable that it almost took on its own character. Some evenings there would be a glow – although never very strong – and on others it would be fading away to almost nothing.

There was a mix of Spanish, Jewish and English residents in the town and our different traditions existed in harmony with one another. Muslims, Christians and Jews lived together: mutually respectful and tolerant. Next door to my family home was a synagogue. The Spanish and Jewish residents tended to work as tradesmen, craftsmen or owned small businesses. The English, in contrast, tended to be richer and more eccentric.

Beginnings

They added an exotic, cosmopolitan flavour but were generally kindly. The rest of the community liked both to work *for* them and to talk *about* them.

I treasure these beautiful memories of my youth. I often think how simple life was then. No computers, no mobiles, only black and white television – and so many books. People were kind, caring and honest. Our neighbours were like family. I remember that, when I did not like my mother's food, I would go to eat with our neighbours. One of the things I loved to do was to walk by the beach on a summer evening with my friends, on the street named Pasio. Dressing up and walking up and down the Pasio was a simple yet exciting event for us young girls and boys. I also loved fashion and, though we could afford little, I knew very well how to manage to look good and attractive even with the very few clothes that I had.

Once a year came my treat of treats – our annual holiday in Tangier. Forty-five kilometres from my home, the city of Tangier was a place of excitement and elegance, international in both character and intrigue. I used to stay with relatives in a popular area, not far from the centre. I would walk endlessly around the city, amazed by the spectacle of the busy metropolitan life that was so different from my small, humble home town. My favourite pastime was to sit beside my mother at the Wall of Lazy People, at the corner of the Boulevard Pasteur, where we could watch the people walking by and the boats leaving for Spain.

Neither of my parents had been educated but they gave us children an education and I fought hard to achieve good results at school. My favourite subjects were literature and French at primary school and English at secondary school. Learning was important to me and I look back proudly on those school days that made me who I am now. At eighteen, I took the baccalaureate to go to university. There I studied literature.

Naima

Looking back, I see that my family didn't have much when I was growing up, but we were content. I sometimes miss those days when we were young and happy with our lot and nothing else mattered. My brothers were fiercely protective over me even when we were children, and we were always incredibly close. Abdeslam was my real guardian when I was very young and, in many ways, still is. From childhood he took care of me and protected me. We all acknowledged that we had come from a humble background, but all three of us had dreams of achieving great success. My brothers and I believed that with sheer, hard work all things were possible.

In keeping with our culture's traditions, my brothers were instrumental in my choice of husband and so I married my husband with their blessing. Marriage meant that I did not complete my degree. Learning had always been such an important thing to me that this has remained a regret, and I think this is the reason why I now place so much importance on education and have always wanted my children to study for their own degrees.

Marriage also meant a new life – far away, in England. My husband and I settled in Victoria in London and it was here that I became a housewife and then a mother when my eldest daughter, Sawsan, was born. Tesco replaced the Thursday market. The rainy streets of London replaced the sun-soaked streets of my home in Morocco. I had passable English when I arrived in my new home but I was by no means fluent at that time, so I took lessons in Westminster and immersed myself in the city to learn its language and its ways. Another daughter, Sabrina, and then my son, Adam, followed quickly. And then another unexpectedly joined our family. My nephew, Mehdi, the son of my brother Ahmed, came into my care when he was a baby. Mehdi was then and is now, in all respects, my own son. Motherhood came naturally to me.

Beginnings

The four children were fairly close in age, and life soon fell into a comforting rhythm. My husband was not skilful behind the wheel of a car so I became the default driver of our family. I got used to driving in the London traffic – in fact, I came to love it. I was a confident driver and spent mornings shepherding my children to and from school and running errands. Driving gave me independence and allowed me to explore and learn about the city that was now my home. Driving to school, housework, shopping and cooking provided the rhythm of my days.

I had come from a poor family and wanted my children to achieve what I had not been able to do, and so my main objective was their education. After French nursery school, the children all went to the Lycée Français Charles De Gaulle and were brought up to be bilingual – fluent in both French and English.

My relationship with my husband was distant, though, and that meant that I was a mother but not really a wife. We were building a family together, but my husband played a very small role in our day-to-day routines. He used to work through the night and sleep by day, and so I became used to doing things by myself. And the children saw little of their father, which meant that I had to be both mother and father at the same time for them. Despite the disappointment of my relationship with my husband, I found fulfilment seeing my family begin to grow up. I enjoyed it all. I was content.

It was during these early years that I met a neighbour called Mary. Mary was from the north of England but London felt more like her natural home. Mary was spontaneous, passionate, kind and incredibly funny. She worked as a manager in Harrods, having recently ended a bad marriage. We bonded immediately through our love of fashion and style and our shared experiences of bringing up a family. Mary made me roar with laughter from the very first day I met her. She was bold and funny and had an innate strength about her. Her

Naima

strength gave me courage and made me feel like I belonged in this strange new city. Mary was a rock for me in those early days and our friendship would last decades. She was one of the people who made me feel at home in London. It is partly down to her that, since those early days, I have felt both Moroccan and English in equal amounts.

Now that I find my life irrevocably changed by my illness, these memories of the early days in London have become even more precious. Every day I relive some of them as a form of therapy. I have become addicted to nostalgia to escape from the prison of my horrible present. I have one particular, much-loved memory that I often spend hours reliving in my mind from these early days of raising a family in London. It is the memory of a day spent in Hyde Park with my small children – running, playing and having a picnic. Each Sunday we went to a different park and, as a result, my children have been to almost every park in London. I have memories of every single one.

As I was caring for my family in London, my brothers started their lives. My brother Ahmed went to work in the Netherlands, as many Moroccans did then. Ahmed was always interested in football and keen to follow the fortunes of Barcelona. Abdeslam has always been fascinated by history, culture, art, fine furniture and architecture. He reads widely and has always had a keen interest in politics. And so he went to study in Belgium. He had to support himself financially in order to do that, so he worked during the night so that he could study during the day. He could not afford to return to Morocco during his university holidays. Instead, he used to go to stay with my brother Ahmed in the Netherlands.

When Abdeslam graduated from Mons Catholic University, he went back to Morocco. There he became a tax inspector in Tangier. Family circumstances meant that the entire responsibility of our wider family fell on his shoulders. He

Beginnings

embraced this and took it as a challenge to help and improve the family's circumstances. Ahmed returned to Morocco and the two of them worked together to change our future.

It was during the eighties that my brothers bought and established a fish restaurant on a cliff top near to Tangier. The location was right above the Cave of Hercules, directly overlooking the expanse of the ocean with a unique and spectacular view along the coastline to our hometown of Asilah. It is a most beautiful location.

Tangier has always been central to my life. As a child, my holidays there were the great excitement of my life. In comparison to Asilah, the city seemed like the centre of sophistication and metropolitan life, and indeed it certainly was. With its history of occupation by the Spanish and briefly by the English, Tangier has a heady mixture of cultures. It is where Africa meets Europe and the Atlantic meets the Mediterranean. It is a fusion of Moroccan and European cultures as a result of its earlier status as a special International Zone until the sixties. For many centuries, Tangier has been home to a vibrant Jewish community whose impact is reflected in schools, synagogues, cemeteries and monuments. And the different communities in the city live in harmony. For me, Tangier has always been a place of peace and tolerance.

The city has attracted talented and famous people from around the world. The painters Delacroix and Matisse were absorbed by Orientalism here, as was the Scottish painter James McBey, whose work my brother Abdeslam admires greatly. Writers have come to Tangier including Jack Kerouac, Tennessee Williams and William Burroughs – and also the writer of *The Sheltering Sky*, Paul Bowles, who befriended my brother Ahmed. Then the city attracted celebrities and designers like Yves St Laurent, Jean-Louis Scherrer, Barbara Hutton and the Rolling Stones.

Naima

One of my favourite films is *Casablanca*, and I like to think that Rick's bar from the movie is somewhere in Tangier. Perhaps it was based on Dean's Bar or the Cinema Vox Bar. Today, I still find the place absorbing with its mixture of modern boulevards and older steep and winding streets, and its constant flow of people.

My brothers' venture was a great success and they soon built up an exciting clientele. With the success of the restaurant, they were able to set up an English pub in the city centre. This generated income that we used to develop the clifftop site into a small hotel to cater for a niche market amongst the increasing number of tourists coming to Tangier.

We started building slowly. First, we renovated the restaurant and brought in new chefs who improved the menu. The revamped restaurant started to attract more regular visitors and tourists. Next, we built nine bungalow suites for residential stays. We were aiming for an exclusive market in the beginning, but soon found that we were regularly booked up. We decided to expand after that, but we wanted to keep to the original idea of luxury, privacy and a warm welcome. We called the resort Le Mirage.

As word of mouth spread about the unique nature and privacy of Le Mirage, we very quickly attracted some famous guests. The success of the venture meant we could look at being even more ambitious. We built more bungalow suites around a swimming pool, and larger suites that directly overlooked the sea. The site was held together by the position of the original restaurant as a focal point, with its terrace fronting the ocean. Le Mirage reflects Abdeslam's eye for the beautiful architecture and decoration, which complement the grandeur of the setting.

Despite achieving such success, my brothers remained humble and grounded. They never forgot who they were or where they came from and remained very proud of their roots and their

Beginnings

past. Sadly, it was just as Le Mirage began to enjoy success that I began to become increasingly concerned about my health. I often joke with my brothers that the money came too late and that I would have liked to have been able to spend some of it in happier times – because my life was about to change irrevocably.

Today, thinking of my past both comforts me and, at the same time, makes me terribly sad – because I cannot have those times back again. And the saddest thing is that these souvenir memories are even more precious, because my life of vitality is not even remotely the same as it was. And I know that nothing can change that.

When things changed

In one way, I am happy to be able to write about the most frightening experience of my life. Deep inside, I have been sad and have felt myself slowly destroyed during these years of suffering with MND, but I feel I gain some power back in being able to tell my story.

We all know that life is full of surprises – sometimes good, sometimes bad. Sadly, the surprise that life had for me was very bad and made my life challenging in a way I could never have imagined. I was born fit and healthy and had lived a strong, healthy and ambitious life. It had never entered my mind that I would not be able to look after my children, my family or others – never mind myself. I had always thought that I would age just like my parents, who were fortunate to remain fit, active and well until later years. I trusted that I had their genes. I have never smoked or touched alcohol and have always maintained a healthy lifestyle and diet. And yet, there came a moment for me when all that began to slip away and change. Motor Neurone Disease completely ambushed me. To suddenly become disabled is the most horrible thing that can happen to anyone. Despite everything, I still find myself asking *why me?*

In 1993, I was bringing up four children when I began to realise that parts of my body were weakening. The decline started in my fingers. I started to lose my grip, and lose control over the movement of my hands. It was more than something that could be explained away as a sprain or an injury. It honestly felt terrifying. But I tried to ignore the issues I was having with my hands for some time. I told myself that it had to be temporary and that my fingers would return to normal. But after a few weeks of waiting and experiencing no improvement, I became increasingly worried and decided to see my general practitioner, Dr. Mitchell. He reassured me and told me that I was far too young to have had a stroke, which might have caused this kind of symptom. His analysis was a sort of relief. And, at the time, I refused to contemplate that this could be anything serious or that it would get worse. I was a busy mother and I had to focus on my children. So, I carried on, confident that things would right themselves somehow. But things didn't right themselves. And then there came the day that I realised that I could not do up my son's shoelaces.

At that moment I panicked. It was the simplest of tasks – one that I had carried out countless times – and my hands would not perform it. It started to feel as though my body was no longer my own. I had spent so many months driving down the fear of what was happening to me and hoping that things

When things changed

would return to normal, but in that moment, I couldn't deny it any more. Something was dreadfully wrong. I went back to my doctor, who referred me to a specialist at Westminster and Chelsea Hospital. There I saw Dr. Gibberd, the consultant neurologist, who examined me and asked for some tests to be done. I waited anxiously for the results. When they came back, they were normal. Again, I felt relief but this time it was tinged with a foreboding. I knew that what was happening to me wasn't normal. It felt as though the tests were failing to give me an answer to a question I needed the answer to, and I simply couldn't allow myself to be reassured. Deep in my mind, I still knew that something wasn't right.

With the tension between the lack of a medical diagnosis and the undeniable sensation of my failing fingers, I became confused and anxious. I almost went into a state of denial because I chose not to tell anybody about what was happening to me – not even my brothers. I was hoping against hope that time would see my symptoms disappear and that there would be no need to worry them. As a result, I had no one with whom to share my worries. I felt utterly alone and started to struggle to sleep. To try and avoid the negative thoughts coming into my head, I distracted myself and remained occupied with the children. They were still young. Sawsan was only nine years old – she was bright and shy and I was so proud of her top grades at the Lycée. And Adam was just three. I felt an enormous weight on my shoulders with the responsibility of four children to raise. I did not want them to know anything about my worries.

So I carried on as normally as possible but, a year later, in 1994, I noticed that my speech had become affected. Articulating words was becoming a struggle and I was having to speak much slower. And the weakness in my fingers – rather than easing – had become much worse. The fear I had been trying to bury deep underneath the reassurances of the test results kept bubbling to the surface. I was losing control of my own body. I decided that I had to have my symptoms reinvestigated, so I went back to see Dr. Gibberd. I was subjected to more tests, including a brain scan, an MRI and a lumbar puncture.

Again I waited anxiously for a few weeks until the results came back. And, again, the results were all normal. This time I was anything but reassured. I knew that *something* was wrong. The tests I had undergone had given me no answers, which frustrated and confused me because I knew my body and *something* was wrong. I became desperate for answers. Dr. Gibberd was also concerned and decided to refer me to one of his colleagues, Dr. Guiloff, for a second opinion.

In the meantime, desperate to turn the tide, I was having acupuncture on a daily basis. I would have tried anything that I thought might heal my mysterious illness. I persevered with the treatment for some time, hoping that it would make a difference. Then one day, I realised that there had been no improvement and that I was just wasting my money. By this stage, I had started to have difficulties with writing and with signing my children's school books. My fingers would often entirely refuse to obey me. I had mixed emotions about this further decline. In the beginning, I would try to find some humour in my clumsiness and used to try and laugh it off. I still didn't know the cause of my symptoms but this, strangely, gave me the strength to carry on hoping that there would be an answer and a cure. I still clung to the hope that one day my fingers would return to normal. I tried fiercely to remain positive. If I did not allow any bad thoughts to enter my mind, I felt that I could remain optimistic. And yet, deep down, I was profoundly worried that I was wrong. I could not fathom that my own body could fail me like this.

One morning in March 1995, I drove my children to school. With me was Habiba. Habiba comes from the small village

When things changed

called Jbilat close to Le Mirage, and she came to work for our family, eventually joining me in London. Habiba never went to school. She also lost one eye as a baby, because of an illness which went untreated. Habiba was more than an employee, though. I considered her a sister, friend and counsellor. I was glad she was with me that day because I was on my way to see Dr. Guiloff for an arranged appointment at Charing Cross Hospital. He had news for me.

It was a cloudy day and, as I drove, I felt excited to find out some answers and to finally get some treatment for my lazy fingers. Despite my darkest thoughts, I was still not totally willing to contemplate that this was anything that couldn't be solved. Inside the hospital, Habiba and I waited in the waiting area. After a few minutes, I was called in. I motioned for Habiba to stay in the waiting room. As I entered the office, Dr. Guiloff welcomed me. I noted his forced smile, and some of my positive thinking waivered because I saw that there was something very serious that he needed to tell me. In that moment, I let the darkest fears I'd tried to keep hidden wash over me. I was scared.

"You have some news for me, sir?" I asked, when I'd sat down.

Dr. Guiloff took a deep breath and I held mine.

"I believe you may be suffering from Motor Neurone Disease," he replied.

"Pardon me, sir, I don't understand. What is that?" I asked.

Dr. Guiloff took off his glasses. He pulled up his chair so he was sitting close to me. He began to tell me everything that he knew about Motor Neurone Disease and I listened with my fear mounting. He quietly told me that the disease ultimately led to paralysis and eventual death. Nobody knew what caused it and, he told me, there was no cure. As he spoke, I struggled to stay calm. I could barely comprehend that this was happening. By the time that he had finished his explanation, I had burst into tears.

"How long do I have left?" I asked.

Naima

"Patients with this condition usually have a maximum of five years," was his reply.

"I have four children, sir," I told him. "They have only me. I have to fight for them."

I still have no idea how, but I pulled myself together and left the room. I was terribly upset and literally shaking, but I pretended to be brave as I left the office and wiped the tears from my eyes. Habiba was waiting outside, desperate for any news. But I brushed her off. I couldn't face telling her about what had been said. I think I had barely taken it in myself. I knew that if I uttered a single word of what I'd been told, I would break down in tears again. I dropped her off and then I drove fast to the Lycée to collect my children. Whilst driving I felt a cloud of terrible anxiety overshadow me. And I felt alone – completely alone. I felt as though I was lost in this huge, dark cloud and struggling all alone to escape from it. A monster was chasing me. The smell of death followed me now.

But then, as I pulled up at the Lycée, Sawsan, Sabrina and Mehdi were waiting for me. When I saw them, I knew that I had to carry on. *I have to fight for them*, I thought. *And I will. And I will win this battle if God wills it.*

That evening, I was on autopilot. My husband was out working as usual. I helped the children with their homework and we talked about what had happened at school that day. I fed them dinner and got them get ready to go to sleep. I tucked my children into their beds and watched their eyes softly close as they fell into sweet dreams. Then, I went to my own bedroom and locked myself inside. And there, I cried and cried and cried.

When things changed

I will never forget that night. My body chills when I think of it, even today. I now knew the truth of what was happening to my body but I didn't want to accept it. I couldn't comprehend what I had been told. I had put myself in a state of denial for so long. Now I couldn't deny what I had learned. I thought about my children and I started to build up a mental wall. I would not give in to MND. It would not define me. That night I made the decision not to tell my children's father about my diagnosis. Our relationship had grown more distant and complicated and I knew he wouldn't be able to support me in the way I needed. I knew that it was up to me to keep on looking after the children and find a way to keep going.

Dominating my every thought from this moment on was the fear of leaving my children when they were all at such a young age. And there was Mehdi – my special, unexpected son – I had promised my beloved brother I would always look after him. I had a very simple dream for my life: I wanted to be able to raise my beloved children and keep them safe. That dream now felt like it was shattering. My life had started to crumble within those few minutes in Dr. Guiloff's office. It felt as though my life had broken into pieces.

Yet my determination not to be cowed by this kept me going in those early days. I focused on the future and somehow found it within myself to carry on as normal in the days that followed. I focused intensely on my children. *They* were the reason for me to fight. My main fear was of leaving them and so I made a silent promise every day, to myself and to my family, that I would hang on to my life for as long as possible. At that time, my children had plenty of activities after school and at the weekend. There were piano lessons, tennis, karate classes and ballet dancing. I was consumed by my children and securing their futures, and I had no time to waste contemplating what was happening to me.

Of course, my symptoms did not miraculously improve, but they remained, thankfully, stable for almost a year. And so, for some time, I managed to continue to hide my condition from both my family and friends. The diagnosis stayed my secret for some time. Looking back, perhaps I felt like I needed time to come to terms with it myself before I burdened my family with it. It was important to me that I appeared completely normal to them and so I became an expert at hiding my worries and my physical struggles. I had to make some practical adjustments but I made sure that no one noticed. For example, I wrapped Sellotape around my car key multiple times to make it larger and therefore easier for me to handle. I used to hide it in my pocket, so that no one would see my modification.

There came a time, though, when it became impossible to hide my condition from my beloved brothers. I finally found the strength to tell them about Dr. Guiloff's diagnosis. My brothers knew me better than anyone and they had known, in their hearts, that something was wrong. They were nevertheless shocked and deeply upset by my revelation. Like me, they had never contemplated that it could possibly be something so serious. But – always my protectors – they immediately rallied around me. It was an oddly confusing moment for me emotionally. I felt relieved to have finally told them my secret and I finally wasn't alone in knowing what was happening to me. But I also felt profoundly sad that I had had to tell my brothers something so upsetting.

We decided that it would be good for me to see another specialist to get another opinion. This time it was Dr. Jeffrey Gawler at a clinic in London. He asked for more tests to be done

When things changed

for various conditions. Again, the results all came back normal. I couldn't help but reach for that slender sliver of hope that this offered. It didn't change what was undeniably happening to my body but maybe could there be another cause? Was it possible that Dr. Guiloff's diagnosis had been wrong? Was it possible that I was suffering from something else – something that had a cure or at least effective treatment and that wouldn't mean I would have to leave my beloved family?

After a few further visits, Dr. Gawler – who was always very kind and humane – advised me to see another famous specialist at Columbia Hospital in New York. Dr. Gawler's secretary, Carmen, would arrange an appointment for me at the hospital in America. Whilst we waited for arrangements to be made, my brother decided to find out more about the American specialist I was being referred to. In doing so, he was introduced by a friend to Dr. Malih. Dr. Malih had been diagnosed with Motor Neurone Disease and he had visited the same specialist in America that I had been referred to. Dr. Malih told my brother that, upon meeting the American specialist, he had quickly been recommended to see his colleague who was based in Paris. This man, Professor Vincent Meininger was the leading expert in the disease and he was the person to see. I decided to cancel my trip to America and instead to arrange to go to Paris to see Professor Meininger as soon as he was available.

Unfortunately, it wasn't until 1996 that this was possible. It was my friend's husband, Hervé, a journalist who arranged for me to see Professor Meininger. I was terribly scared about the appointment but I still had that little piece of hope – I *still* thought it might be possible that the doctors had been wrong. I was not able to sleep for the few days before the appointment.

The big day came. My brother and I travelled to Paris from London. I could see that Abdeslam was trying to hide his fear – that I was facing a final and terminal diagnosis – and I knew that he was suffering in silence and trying to be strong for me. We arrived early at La Gare du Nord. There was a group of close friends waiting for us at the Pitié-Salpêtrière university hospital: Tahar Ben Jelloun (the Moroccan novelist), Lotfi Akali, and Hervé who had so kindly pushed for the appointment for me. They all also tried to comfort me by being positive. I joined in with Tahar as we laughed and made jokes. I was also trying to make it appear as though I was not worried. The reality was that I was frightened and I desperately wanted to believe that this was a nightmare that I would wake from. I looked around the beautiful city of Paris and wished fervently that I was there for any other purpose.

We arrived at the hospital and we were told to wait. Then I heard my name.

"Madame Chakkour?"

My heart began to thump and I started shaking. I turned around and there was a man – Professor Meininger – opening the door for me. Trembling uncontrollably, I entered his office. Professor Meininger looked to be an extremely serious and calm person. He invited me to sit close to him, questioned me in a soft voice and examined me in a caring and supportive way. As we spoke he started to refer to a new, more specific diagnosis, ALS: amyotrophic lateral sclerosis.

"Is that the same as MND, sir?" I asked.

"Yes," he replied in a very low voice.

So that was it. Dr. Guiloff hadn't been wrong. The worst was still true.

There in Paris, I had the final diagnosis. No matter how hard I tried now, there was no more denying it. And there was no more hope. I now knew that the form of Motor Neurone Disease that I had was ALS, but it was still a progressive and incurable illness. I knew that it would lead to weakness and wasting of my muscles; it would cause the eventual loss of my mobility; it would take

When things changed

away my power of speech; it would take my independence and then it would take my life.

My last hopes – however real they had ever been – were gone. Again, I felt my whole world collapsing on me and it took me a few minutes to breathe and to regain any strength. Even though I already knew the answer, I asked him the question that was still at the forefront of my mind.

"How long…?"

Before I had finished my sentence, he understood and answered – and he answered in the most diplomatic, sensitive and caring of ways. Life expectancy with ALS is usually two to five years from the start of symptoms. My symptoms had started three years previously. Professor Meininger had told me that my disease was making slow progress and, for that, I counted myself as lucky.

"*La maladie est mechante* [The disease is vicious]," he said. "It is impossible to know the exact time you have left. But we have started to find out more information about this dreadful disease. Hopefully, one day we will be able to find the cure or at least to slow the progression. And at present, we have two new drugs on trial."

I immediately agreed to participate in the trials. And I left the hospital with a prescription of vitamin E and baclofen (a muscle relaxant). I had a string of dates for further appointments and I also had the application form to sign for the experimental new drug called riluzole. If it worked, the doctor told me, it could potentially give me another three months of life expectancy. I had survived three years with this disease already, I thought to myself. Perhaps I would have the time to complete my mission: to see my children grow up.

Naima

After my diagnosis was finally confirmed in Paris, I had to accept that my last hope was destroyed. In those first few weeks, when my children were all asleep, I used to cry thinking about what my future held. But from that day, I also renewed my declared war against my enemy – Mr. Motor Neurone Disease. I also turned to my faith for comfort and found solace there. And I promised my brothers that I would fight this battle, if God so willed I should. I saw clearly that each minute of my life was now more precious than ever, and I promised myself that I would invest all my time and energy into my children. I tried to have a plan for maximising each day I had, focusing on my priority, which was always my children and their education. Knowing that I had only a short time made me hungrier to see them safe, successful, happy and set up for their adult lives. The knowledge that my life would be much shorter than I had ever anticipated hung over me like a cloud but, in a way, that actually strengthened me and gave me a tremendous energy to keep fighting. Every hour was now very important. The race against time had begun for me.

This is the reality...
What does it feel like to have MND?

I have always had a great affinity with the sea. I grew up beside it and used to swim in the waves as a child. It is the sea that I return to when I go to our home in Tangier. When I was given my diagnosis I felt as though I became something like a sea. On the surface – especially at first when I was in denial and keeping it a secret from my loved ones – it appeared as if nothing had changed and the waters were still and calm. Determined to keep my children protected from the truth for as long as possible, I maintained that calm outer surface for a while. Nobody who laid eyes on me would have any reason to suspect that beneath my serene surface were tumults of fear as well as moments of sheer despair, sadness and fury that my life had been hijacked by this vicious condition.

My immediate fear upon diagnosis was my death – and my children losing their mother. I consider myself lucky that the disease progressed slowly at first. And this made it easier to keep my condition a secret from everyone – even my beloved brothers. And it seemed natural to hide my condition for as long as possible to shield my children from the reality of what was happening to me – and so I did. I realise now that I also used this form of denial as a coping mechanism. Part of my way of coping with my worries at that time was keeping my attention focused elsewhere and away from the fears I had. So I kept the surface of myself calm and seemingly untroubled even as my depths were filling with despair. I pushed all my fears down into the ocean underneath. In hindsight, I see that this was not ultimately helpful for me. Indeed, it meant that those first years were very lonely and I had to hold the burden of the knowledge of my condition and all the fear and despair that brought inside myself. And when those emotions inevitably rose in waves to the surface, it felt like it was something I had to endure alone. And that was hard.

Through the years, death eventually became something I feel is inevitable rather than my greatest fear. But eventually – and inevitably – the calm surface I had maintained so carefully and for so long was broken as the physical changes to my body became undeniable. The day came when I could not stand up or walk without help. In that moment, I understood that MND would take so much more than my life. I could only expect worse things to come. From there, my freedom started to disappear bit by bit. The inevitability of it was so frightening, as was the fact that I knew my condition could only get worse.

This is the reality…

When this day came, I was lucky enough to have the help I undeniably needed in the form of Habiba. We had known each other for years but our relationship became more than just a simple friendship, and she became more than just family staff. Habiba had suffered her own physical issues and we became two disabled people together – inseparable. Habiba filled my days with humour and joy, and our relationship became stronger than ever. We understood each other and have continued to have the tightest of human bonds. These days Habiba is my hands and legs. She washes and dresses me and does everything for me as though I am her baby. I realised that God might have made me ill, but He had also sent a truthful person to look after me. God took my health, but He gave me Habiba.

Over the years, I have come to know about many people who were diagnosed at the same time as myself and then passed away only a few months afterwards. Every one of them felt like a loss and reminded me of my own situation. Although I never got to know him, Dr. Malih was one of those people. He was the man who had recommended seeing Professor Meininger. We also shared a mutual friend in Tahar Ben Jelloun. He was one of the first people I knew who also had MND.

In the summer of 1996, he came to stay at Le Mirage in Tangier. I had not yet received my final and definitive diagnosis from Professor Meininger. In many ways, I was still in denial about the reality of what was happening to me. I was still wildly clinging to hope that somehow my own symptoms could be explained in some other way. During that summer, I was asked if I wanted to meet Dr. Malih, but I honestly couldn't bring myself to do it. The physical reality of Dr. Malih's condition at that time was undeniable. For myself, I still clung to hope but I also felt fear. And I couldn't bring myself to meet him because to do so would mean I had to contemplate my own possible future. I just could not accept, at that time, that I had the same illness as him. Although I didn't meet Dr. Malih, I found myself watching him from afar whilst he stayed at the hotel. I now see that my reluctance to face Dr. Malih was a reluctance to accept the truth about my own diagnosis. To look directly at him and see his reality would be to see my own future – and that terrified me. Seeing the reality of what MND could do to a person would have been more than my mind could bear. I felt terrible when I found out that he had passed away a few weeks after this holiday. I wish I had had the courage to speak with him then.

It was during check-ups at King's College Hospital that I finally had to confront the reality of the disease I had. Here, I saw for the first time other Motor Neurone Disease patients at close quarters. In the beginning, I used to avoid looking at other patients with more advanced stages of the disease than me. Again, I found myself not wanting to accept that I had the same illness. I was nervous about being so close to the reality of what I had and what my future looked like. I used to ask for my wheelchair not be placed directly in front of others who were in a much poorer condition than myself. I even tried to close my eyes so as not to see, but I soon found out that hearing the sounds many of them made was much more frightening. Some were struggling to speak to their companions. Some were struggling for breath. I felt so desperately sorry for them but also terrified at the idea that this was what awaited me.

One of the first things to be affected by MND was my hands. It was the weakness in my fingers that was the first sign that something was wrong in 1993. We take our hands for granted. Think of your own hands and all the tasks they carry out each and every day. We lift, grip, push, pull, hold, carry and reach. We scratch when we feel an itch. We use our hands to feed ourselves, to clean ourselves and to wipe away our own tears and the tears of our loved ones. And we stroke, we soothe and reassure with our hands. We use them to hold the hands of our children as

This is the reality...

we walk across a busy road or through a park on a sunny day. We hold the hands of our loved ones when they are sad or sick. Hands are such a vital part of how we exist as human beings. And so I can't stress how frightening even these early changes in my body were. I felt like my own hands were floating away from me – almost leaving me behind. This betrayal by my own body felt like a hammer blow.

One of the next things to be affected was that I started to lose control over my speech – I began stumbling over words and sentences. As this has worsened, I have felt much more than mere frustration at losing my main means of communication. MND was slowly robbing me of my voice – my agency, my means of asserting and defining myself.

Still determined to cover up the changes to my body as best I could, I initially deflected questions about the slurring of my words by explaining that I was taking tablets which affected my ability to talk. On one occasion, I went to collect my daughters from a friend's birthday party. When I arrived at the venue – a very posh place in London – I was stopped by the doormen who thought that I was drunk. This incident upset and embarrassed me, but it also deeply undermined my confidence. I still have a semblance of my voice today but it is something that works against me. I am slow to communicate because every word is an effort. Often, I have to repeat what I say. Good friends who know me well have to translate for me with new people. Every sentence is a huge effort. It is sometimes awful and, honestly, an embarrassment. I try to accept it with humour and laughter but I do not have an infinite supply of these. Losing my voice has been one of the things that has made me rage against the unfairness of it all.

Another thing that MND changed profoundly for me was sleep. Everyone needs good sleep and it has so many health benefits. Restful sleep is important for our brain, immune system and mood. But sleep does not come easy for sufferers of MND. The two parts of the day and night when I am most conscious of my illness and what it has done to me are waking up in the morning and going to sleep at night. Both are a daily ordeal and I have come to hate going to bed as a result. Despite having a pressure-relieving mattress topper and now a water bed, every night I experience terrible pain and, of course, I cannot move myself. I have to be turned and moved regularly during the course of the night. Poor Habiba with her short legs has to jump on my bed and pull and turn me to ease the soreness and pain in my body. If my night could be filmed, it would be a tragicomedy. I have also needed an oxygen mask for the last six years to regulate my breathing at night. For many, the promise of a safe bed to rest in at the end of the day is a joy. Not for me. I become panicky and anxious when it becomes dark because I dread bedtime so much. I know that I will lie awake – restless and in pain – into the small hours, until finally I find sleep for maybe two or three hours. I don't think I can remember the last time I had a truly restful night's sleep. I sometimes ask myself "How the hell have I managed to survive all these years without really, *truly* sleeping?"

When sleep does come, I often dream that I am running. In my dreams, sometimes I am running in the streets of Asilah, and sometimes I am running in London. My ability to walk or to run has been gone for several years and yet I still have these recurring dreams. At first, I was puzzled by them, but I think that it is my mind adjusting to my illness. I am sure that these kinds of dreams are experienced by many MND sufferers. The worst thing about them is the return to reality upon awakening. I wake after these dreams and realise, over and over again, that it was just a dream and that I cannot walk or move without help. It's like waking from a sweet dream to a nightmare.

This is the reality…

Today, when people see me in a wheelchair, my condition is undeniable. Yet people will still often just see the surface of me. They will often praise me for being brave, for being resilient and uncomplaining or for being a "fighter" against this terrible disease. Even today, there are depths of my experience and emotions that I try to keep hidden and that it is impossible for others to fathom unless they look below the surface. Imagine, for a moment, waking from a night where you have barely found sleep to a world where you don't have the use of your limbs. You don't have your voice, and communication is a daily struggle. You cannot feed yourself. You cannot wipe your own nose or wipe your own tears away. You cannot reach out and hold a child or grandchild. That is my reality now. And the reality of so many others suffering with MND. But I do not consider myself an MND warrior or a hero. I feel more like an MND victim. I have moments of despair. I have moments where I find it impossible to find any hope. And I have moments of anger – anger that *I* have been selected by God or Fate to suffer this way.

Some years ago, my beloved Mehdi got married and a videographer came to capture the day on film. We watched it together as a family, but later that evening, I watched it again – alone, with just Habiba keeping an eye on me as she always does. This time, I found myself moved to tears. And this time the tears weren't of joy at seeing my son so happy… they were of profound sadness. I cried because I saw something in video that perhaps nobody else did. I rarely see myself in the mirror and here, on screen, I saw myself as I now was. I saw what Motor Neurone Disease had done to me physically. The pressure of the mask that helps me breathe at night has now permanently left its mark on my face. There is a deep, noticeable scar around my mouth. It has destroyed my confidence and now I hate the look of my face. I try to hide it with the best brand foundations but I find that still nothing works for me. Motor Neurone Disease has not only taken my mobility, my voice, and my independence, but the mask that I need to help me breathe has permanently reshaped my face. I also saw how my body had changed shape and how much of the woman I once was has now gone. Watching myself on that wedding video was like standing before a mirror that I never wanted to be reflected in because I did not recognise the woman in the footage. It was almost as if I were looking at an entirely different person. I cried for what I had lost that night – my old self. The day of the wedding is a wonderful memory but that footage hurt me deeply on a level that few people can understand; because that is the true reality of Motor Neurone Disease. It robs you of yourself. It strips everything from you.

I am grateful for the years that I have been gifted. In 1993 I was told I had five years maximum and yet I have had many more. In 2021, we were together, on the beach at Tangier, as a family. The sun was shining and the sea was a crystal blue. It was a beautiful day. I was remembering swimming in the sea as a young girl and I suddenly had the urge to touch the water. I asked Mehdi to push me into the waves so I could feel the ocean. My wheelchair was customised so it could not be damaged by the seawater and I knew that my funny Mehdi would agree to my latest crazy idea. My shoes were pulled off and my trousers folded up above my ankles. Both Mehdi and Adam pushed me gently towards the water until I could feel the cool, lapping waves over my toes and then the sea foam licking up my ankles. It was the first time I had physically touched the sea for thirty years. I threw my head back and laughed. I soaked up the moment and also the laughter and happiness of my family as they watched me. And yet, even this golden moment was marred by sadness. I felt a pang that I wasn't walking into the sea holding my sons' hands or the hands of my grandchildren. Even on this beautiful day, in that wonderful place and surrounded by my loving family – that was still something that had been stolen from me by this disease.

This is the reality...

I have tried, through the years, to maintain the surface of myself and keep the rage and the despair under my calm waters. I have never wanted to burden those around me with my pain and fears. This can sometimes be exhausting. Everybody understands the familiar feeling of tiredness when welcome-but-energetic guests unwittingly overstay their welcome. You love their company but tiredness makes your eyes drop as you gaze at the clock, wondering when they will head home and you can be quiet again. I often feel that tiredness now, and it is a tiredness that I never experienced before MND. It's a tiredness beyond the tiredness of a mother of four children. It's hard to convey this to friends, whose company I love, especially when they see my nearly-always-present smile. And when people ask me, it's hard to convey the weight of the pain, fear and – yes – anger that I carry as a result of what MND has done to me. I know it is not anyone else's burden to carry. It is mine. But somehow, I still want to let others see beneath the calm surface I work so hard to maintain, and to see the reality of MND. Because it's important that we look at the truth and recognise it for what it is.

Raising a family
in the shadow of MND

Back in 1996, at the time of my final and definitive diagnosis, my eldest daughter, Sawsan, was just eleven and in sixième at the Lycée Charles de Gaulle. My wish, at that moment, was to see her obtain the baccalaureate and to start at university, so that she could then oversee the education of her younger sister and brothers if I was no longer there. That was what my mission was.

It was my conscious choice not to initially reveal to my children the truth about my diagnosis or the nature of the disease. They were all still so young. I did not want them to see my pain or become frightened about what was happening to me. I wanted to protect them from the distressing reality of my illness. If I'm entirely honest, I also wasn't sure *how* I could possibly share that reality with them. How do you tell children that their mother is dying? How could I explain to them that there was no cure and nothing that the doctors could do to make me better? So I tried for as long as possible to shield my children. I did my best not to show my struggles with my weakening body. Even on days when I might have looked physically weak, I made sure my head was held high and showed them that my spirit remained strong. I constantly told them that nothing could break their mummy.

I tried hard to never show any sign of weakness or sadness, but children have a way of sensing when things aren't right. I couldn't hide the decline in my condition from them forever and it eventually became obvious that their mother was unwell. This caused them deep anxiety which I did my best to soothe. Whilst I couldn't hide the fact that I was ill, for a long time they didn't know that I was terminally ill.

What I did have – and continue to be profoundly grateful to God for – was the support and love of my brothers. As my diagnosis became my new reality, Le Mirage was becoming more and more successful. Our family had come from humble beginnings but my brothers' hard work was paying off. I do not speak lightly when I say that Abdeslam and Ahmed sacrificed their own wants and needs entirely to provide the care they knew I needed. My brothers didn't just put their own lives on hold when they learned about my condition – they put me above themselves. I am not exaggerating when I say that everything my brothers have done since my diagnosis has been for me. By 1996, my needs were already changing and no expense was spared in finding the best care for me so that I could live life as normally as possible for as long as possible with my children.

Raising a family in the shadow of MND

My brothers and I have always been close but friends are still impressed and surprised by the energy with which they came to my aid. Some have remarked on the extraordinary bond the three of us share, and it's something I've always been grateful for. Materially, I have wanted for nothing. But I always say that I would give up all the money our family has – everything we own – just for a life free from MND.

In the early years whilst my symptoms developed blessedly slowly, my children took up all my energy and, like any family, they could be emotionally exhausting. Since becoming a mother, my priority in life has always been the education and healthy development of my children. I know that this will be a familiar desire for many parents. When my everyday life was easier for me to manage through small adaptations to my regular activities, they were what I built my days around.

On school days, I would get up every day at seven and dress, with the help of Habiba, who had by then become an almost constant companion to me. She was my hands when mine were failing me. She was constantly by my side to help me in my mission to raise my children. I would make sure that all my children had a proper breakfast. Then we would pile the children into the car and Habiba would help me into the driver's seat and put the safety belt on me. The car was an automatic-drive and I would start the engine with my specially adapted key. It was important for me to drive my children to school for as long as I was able to. Driving my children to school gave me an injection of normality, a sense of independence, and made me feel like a "normal" mother. It was a time of the day I really treasured.

Whilst driving them to their day's lessons, I would revise multiplication with Sabrina and Mehdi. Both Sabrina and Mehdi required a great deal of supervision in their studies. I would drop the children outside the school and Sawsan would take her younger siblings to their sections at the Lycée. When I

Naima

returned home, Habiba would be waiting for me by the window so that she could help me out of the car. I'd then watch TV for an hour and read the news, whilst Habiba did some housework.

Some people are surprised when they find out I was driving with my diagnosis. But they say that if you really try, you can solve any problem. And I've found ways to overcome the obstacles that my illness has thrown at me over the years – especially when it came to raising my children. I found ways of adapting to the changes my body was going through so that I could still carry out everyday tasks. People who knew of my diagnosis were often fascinated by the vast range of things that I could still do and achieve despite my illness. I was always keen to ensure I was no different from other mothers. This meant constantly adapting my workable daily routine as my own capabilities changed. I carried on acting as normally as possible. I focused on my children *all* of the time – pushing thoughts of the disease and what it was doing to me to the back of my mind. It was important to me that I was a strong mum, always ready to help and to protect them from anything. I was determined that the disease would not prevent me from doing that.

But when my condition worsened, I began to struggle. My daily routine became more challenging and it became more difficult to maintain my pretence to my children that everything was normal. The reality was that my body was becoming weaker and I was losing the ability to carry out the everyday tasks that had been the rhythm of my days.

When my children were older and I felt they were ready, I told them the truth. I told them that I had Motor Neurone Disease. What it would eventually do to me. And I told them that it was incurable and that it would eventually lead to my death. This is still one of the hardest things I have ever had to find the words for. With hindsight, I think my children's characters have been strengthened by this experience. They found the strength to understand and accept what has happened to me. I also think they've learned new skills in resilience by watching how I have dealt with the challenges of my illness. They have also learned to focus on what is really important in life and to appreciate everything they have.

I never missed any of my children's school meetings at the Lycée or at Collingham Sixth Form College where they went on to study afterwards. I remember one particular meeting which I was determined to attend. Mehdi was struggling that year and I had to speak with his teachers about how we could improve his progress. I was worried that they might make him repeat the year. Of course, I wanted to encourage Mehdi in any way we could so he could avoid the embarrassment of having to resit with younger students whilst his friends advanced. But, always in the back of my mind was the worry about losing time in the race with my illness. I couldn't afford to miss this meeting. That day, though, I had a horrible cold and a runny nose. For most people this would not be an issue; they would have simply armed themselves with a tissue and headed into the meeting. But at that point I was losing even more use of my hands and arms and so my situation was more complicated. Whilst talking with Mehdi's teachers, I found my nose was dripping all the time. I had to turn repeatedly to Habiba, who was sitting beside me, so she could dab it with a tissue. Things got even worse when my chewing gum became stuck on my lip during the course of the meeting. The teachers were very sympathetic. They saw how worried I was about my son. Happily, Mehdi made improvements and was able to carry on and advance into the next year.

Like any mother, my relationships with my children haven't always been easy. I'll admit that I was a strict parent. Perhaps this was just in my nature as I am Muslim and from a conservative social background. Or perhaps it was the added pressure I felt

Naima

from my failing body and the time I felt ticking away. I couldn't afford for anything to go wrong. I needed to make sure my children would be all right if I was suddenly not around. Sawsan was more self-motivated at school than her siblings but I still felt that all my children needed someone behind them all the time to push them onwards. That was what I tried to do.

I have tried to make sure that my children have mixed with good people. As a result, I had conflicts with some of their friends whose behaviour I did not like. I have always believed that mixing with bad company leads to disaster and I couldn't risk that for my children. Again, perhaps because of my Muslim heritage I was particularly aware of the dangers of a big city like London where there is so much freedom and there are so many temptations for young people. I have to confess that, when it came to caring for my daughters in particular, I was especially vigilant. I used to follow their activities closely – so closely that it almost amounted to spying on them. I felt that the world was too risky a place for them to be left alone. I used to drive with Habiba to their favourite places to see who they were meeting. Poor Habiba! Sometimes I forced her to go inside to check and report back. Habiba hated doing this, but she did it because she knew that I could not do it myself and she understood that my worries about my children were real.

My children started to play tennis at a very young age. For several years they also used to travel to the famous tennis camp of Bollettieri in Florida and to Bruguera in Spain. One day I began to see some strange behaviour on the part of my daughters' female coach. Sawsan was fourteen and Sabrina only twelve. The coach used to invite young girls, including my daughters, to expensive restaurants and to hang out with them all the time. I felt it was very inappropriate behaviour for an adult coach and her students. To begin with I mentioned it to their father, but he did not want to pursue the matter. Then, one day after being with their coach, Sabrina and Sawsan came home *very* late: it was midnight. I was very angry. So angry that I decided to leave them outside despite the cold and the rain, until their father returned from work and let them inside. They had been with the tennis coach. I called the coach the next day and asked her not to approach my daughters any more. She was shocked and worried about what I would do. She was right to be, as I gave her phone number to the headmistress of the Lycée, where many of her students attended. The headmistress called her to tell her to keep away from the students at her school. She made her aware of the dangerous consequences if she did not. A few weeks later, when she left the club, I was relieved.

Every single thing that I have been through and that I have done has been to prepare my children for a positive future. And I understood that some of the things I did for them, they would only appreciate when they, too, became parents. I was brought up to believe that the mother is the first teacher, the one who prepares a child to be a good and honest person in society. The mother should be a good example for her children in every aspect of life. And that is what I have tried to be for mine. This became more of a challenge as my relationship with their father fell apart.

In every human life there are things that should not be revealed or discussed with anyone. Nobody is owed your whole truth and so there are some darker secrets of my struggle with MND that I will hold inside and these will go to the grave with me. This book, whilst written for my children, will also hopefully be read by others as I want the world to pay more attention to the disease that has taken over my life. I want people who are suffering with their own diagnoses to find some hope or at least comfort in these pages. But some family matters, which are very personal, I will not include here in my story – such as arguments and crises with my children. And I will also not speak in detail about how my husband reacted to my diagnosis. But I will tell you how our marriage ended.

Our relationship had always been distant, but after my diagnosis and the start of the deterioration of my body, I recognised that my husband's attitude had changed for the worse. His behaviour towards me and his children became aggressive and intolerable once my illness became physically apparent. We had not had a good relationship for a long time but I was still shocked and confused by his strange attitude. I had already realised that he was not a person that I could rely on for help and support, which was why I had hidden my diagnosis from him for some time. But I now had a different image of him in my mind. As my condition worsened, he seemed to slowly detach himself from me and from our family. He spent less time with the children and was absent from, more than present in, our home. Subsequently, my own emotional detachment from him and from our marriage grew. Our marriage, such that it was, was something that I did not have time for in my life now that I felt a clock was ticking. The relationship fell apart.

It was ultimately my husband's choice to leave the family and our home. Even though our relationship had already effectively ended, I have never understood how someone can abandon or hurt a person who is seriously ill and at their most vulnerable. But an illness like MND takes a great toll on even the most devoted marriages. In my experience, some men seem to be much more likely than women to leave a relationship when their spouse becomes seriously ill. This was certainly true for me.

When I married, I believed it was for life – come what may. I had been raised to be faithful and I am loyal to my family and the people I love and care for. The complicated truth is that, had it not been for my life-changing illness, there is a real chance that my husband and I might have unhappily stayed together for life.

After he left, my children kept me going and I came not to care about his absence. Again, my brothers stepped in to help me make sure our little family was cared for, whilst I managed to find a way to keep going. By 2006, however, I had reached the point where I could no longer bear being legally married to him. He had taken no further interest in the family or myself since he had left – essentially leaving me as a single parent. I saw then that so much of our marriage had been built on the sacrifices *I* had made. And now I was also at a point where I needed to take back control. I was losing control over my own body and so I felt the visceral need to take hold of the control I *did* have over my circumstances. So I did. Some might take the view that the choice to begin my marriage wasn't entirely my own because of our arranged marriage, but I certainly made the choice to end it. I filed for divorce.

The decision to divorce my husband was not one that I took lightly. Divorce is not accepted widely in my culture and it was with great unhappiness that I filed the papers. Yet I was convinced it was the right thing, for both myself and my children. Unfortunately, our divorce was a nasty, long and painful experience. My husband did his best to make the process as hard as possible. There were frequent trips to the court and some ugly letters from my husband's lawyer. For me, it was an emotional rollercoaster. Even though, by this time, my children were not little any more, our divorce both affected and hurt them – especially my youngest son, Adam. I was, by then, struggling with my speech, and my husband petitioned the court to stop our eldest daughter, Sawsan, from attending court with me to assist with translating my words and making sure I was understood. The meanness behind this request shocked and upset my daughter more than it did me. Sawsan refused to agree to her father's demands and fought hard to be with me at each court appearance. His action was all the more vindictive, in my view, because I had always been a loyal wife and devoted mother to his children. Although our marriage was over, I had done nothing wrong during the course of our time together. He was the one who had chosen to leave. His animosity left us all scarred.

Once my divorce was finalised, I felt tremendous relief. I am still rather surprised, even today, at the power I felt from that relief. The divorce had been bitter and painful, but I do not regret it for a moment. In fact, I felt that I should have done it a long time before. I am so grateful that God helped me see a way out of the toxic and damaging relationship that was my marriage, and has helped me to recognise the really good relationships in my life.

It's an odd thing to contemplate but it is perhaps my personal experience with MND that has shown me which friendships and relationships are *real*. As a religious person, I strongly believe that everything happens for a reason. When I think about what has happened through my life and when I look back over time, I can see that there is a lesson or at least something good has come – no matter how small it might be in comparison to what I am suffering – from every challenge I've faced. Although I would give anything for things to be different, I realise that living with MND has taught me a lot about life. I have become a different person from the person I was before my illness. Sometimes, when I think of the hard times I went through during my marriage and the divorce and how it affected my children, I cry my heart out. But I also feel proud of myself because, in those moments, I took charge of my own life and my own identity. I was no longer my husband's wife. I was Naima. I was a mother and I was still here, despite everything.

Raising a family in the shadow of MND

When a serious illness strikes a person, it affects the whole family. It can be the biggest crisis a family goes through. It can break families apart. My marriage did not survive my diagnosis. But my illness only strengthened the relationship I have had with my two brothers. I am fortunate and so thankful for the relationships I have had with my two wonderful brothers – Abdeslam and Ahmed were my soul mates. People have often commented on the closeness of our sibling relationship. I believe that my relationship with my brothers is special and possibly unique. Together, we share our experiences and memories of our modest background in Asilah and the changes that our family has navigated throughout the decades. We went on to have families of our own and they also are incredibly close. Even before my diagnosis, my brothers were always there for myself and my children. Mehdi – my brother's son – is *my* son. I am his mother. The bonds my brothers and I have shared are indissoluble. I speak from the heart when I say that they are the lights of my life.

After my diagnosis and the end of my marriage, our family life changed in major ways. And my beloved brothers made changes to their own independent lives in order to support me and the children both emotionally and financially, especially after their father left. They travelled frequently to London to help me to raise the children and make the adaptations to our living space that were needed to accommodate my changing circumstances. My brothers gave up and abandoned many things, including their own dreams and plans, and they did it for me and my children. They have ensured that any new treatment for my condition was made available to me, and they have keenly watched the world of research into MND. They have never once given up hope that there might be something close to a cure or at least something that would slow my symptoms or ease my pain. Nothing has been left untried. My brothers have never given up on me. And nothing is too much for them when it comes to my children. People often credit me with strength and bravery for living with MND for so many years but I honestly feel that I would not have survived even a day without them. I often frighten myself by imagining a world where I was facing this terrible disease without them. In many ways, the focus of their lives became *me* and that, to me, is real love. They are my heroes. Not a day goes by when I am not grateful to God for having my brothers beside me.

My days now are split between my home in London, my home in Tangier and, in the summer, Le Mirage hotel – the beautiful retreat that my brothers have built. Le Mirage is a spectacular place but it is also a place full of people. I love people. Just like the little girl who liked to sit at the corner of the Boulevard Pasteur in Tangier and watch the passers-by, I still love to watch people. Friends often joke that I am an expert at reading people. I recall sitting with my dear friend, Gerald, for lunch one day at Le Mirage. He was facing the window and the ocean and commented on the "beautiful view". I laughed and looked across the busy, buzzing restaurant full of other people with their chatter and their stories and noted to him that my view wasn't too bad either.

Le Mirage, like Tangier itself, attracts some of the most interesting and accomplished people in the world with its beauty and peaceful atmosphere. I am fortunate to have met many of them. Some of them have become friends for life. Since my diagnosis, I have come to understand the true meaning of friendship. Whilst many of the people in my life are famous, powerful and wealthy, that is not what I look for in friends. I look for sincerity, loyalty and real empathy. We are all humans together at the end of the day, and fame or money does not make any difference. In fact, I strongly believe that money can be a force for bad if it becomes an obsession. It can tear families apart and destroy friendships.

Above: With my friend Mary in London during happy days in 1986.
Left: Young and fit, with my two daughters.

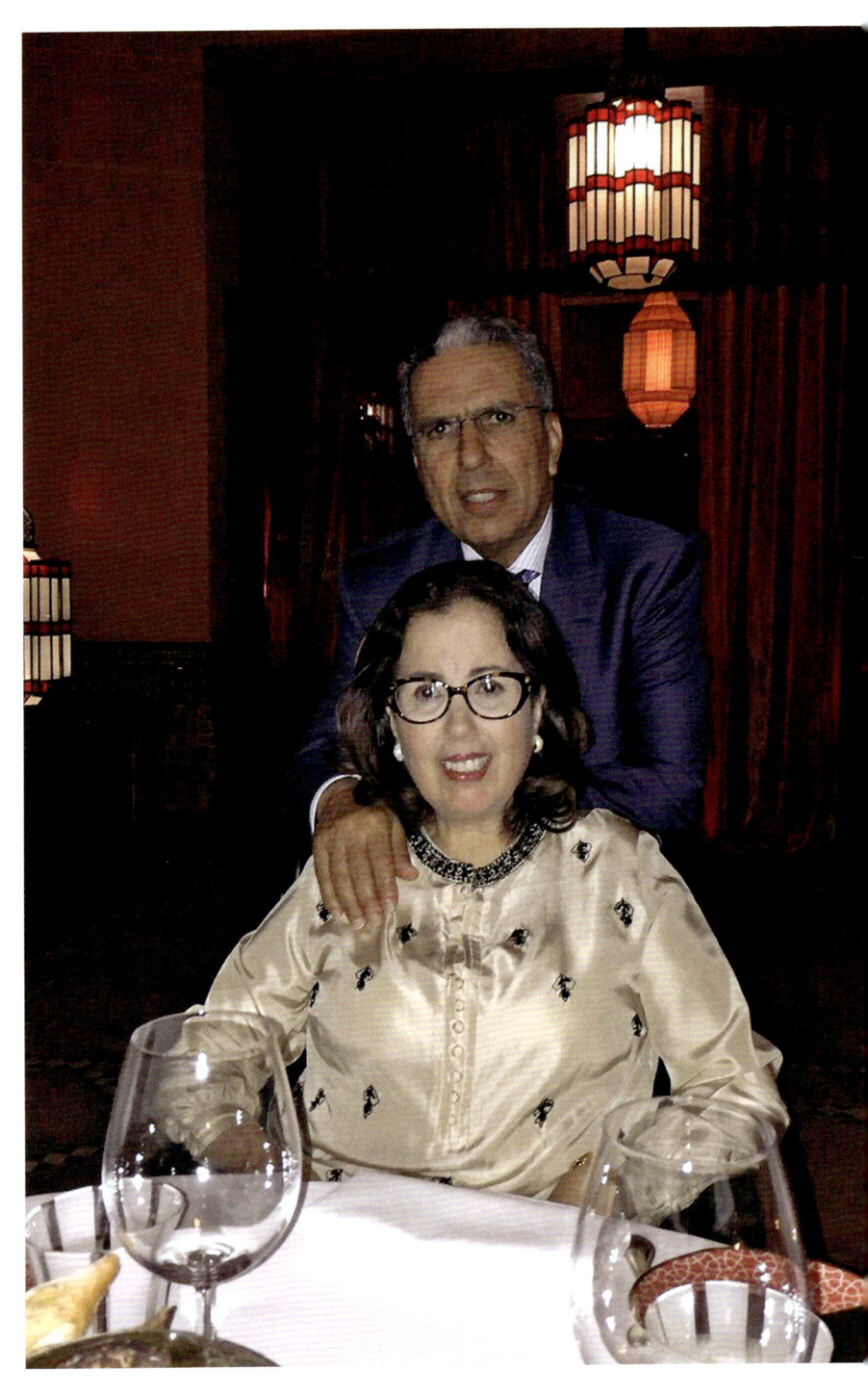

Above: On holiday in Marrakesh with my special and beloved brother, Abdeslam.

Above: With my beloved brother Ahmed outside The White House in 2012.

Left: With my rock, Habiba.
Below: My beautiful daughters, Sawsan and Sabrina.

Above: Summer 2021, with my sons Mehdi and Adam by the sea.

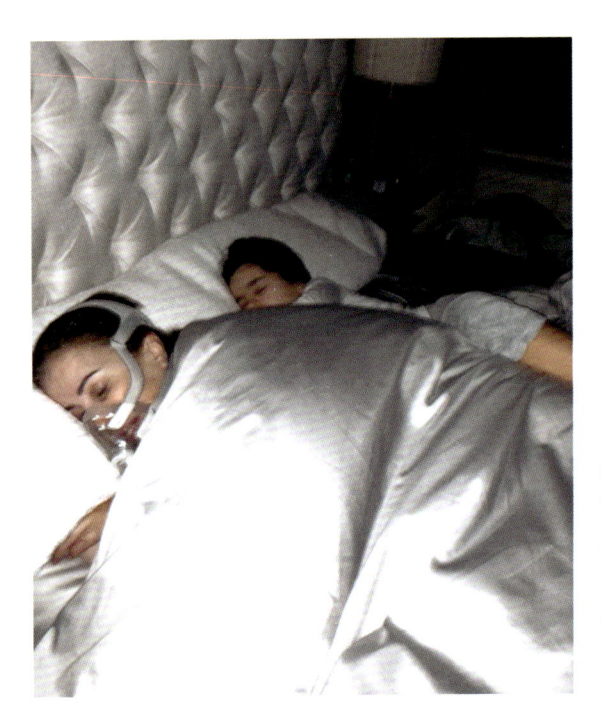

Left: My granddaughter Sofia curled up beside me in bed – one of my best moments.
Below: Brunch at Sawsan's wedding celebrations in 2015.

Left: A family birthday with my grandsons.
Below: Writing my story has been made possible by using a switch on my neck to instruct a computer keyboard. It has been a long but worthwhile process.

Above: My oxygen: my grandchildren in 2024.

Raising a family in the shadow of MND

I have been blessed with and also sadly lost many friends through the years. It is a peculiar sadness to lose friends when you are living with a terminal illness. One such friend was Adolfo de Velasco, an antiques specialist, a keen partygoer, and owner of a beautiful palace in Tangier. He was a real ambassador for Morocco and a true friend. Jean-Louis Scherrer, who was one of our first guests at the hotel and who passed away in 2013, was a great French couturier in the chic Parisian style. He was one of the most loyal and ever-loving of friends. I recall a beautiful afternoon on the terrace having lunch with Gerald when Jean-Louis joined us with his companion Tony. Tony, a rather large man, patted his belly and smiled at me, adding in a low and mischievous whisper, "Don't tell anyone, Naima, but I'm expecting!" I love people who can make me laugh, and Tony did frequently. He would pick up my brother's little dog, Maddox, and kiss him firmly on the lips. I miss Jean-Louis and Tony very much and I am so grateful that they came into my life.

Another individual I am honoured to have as a friend is Felipe González, former Prime Minister of Spain. Felipe is not only a skilful and smart politician, but also has a good heart and is very much a people person. He lives a simple life, even though his popularity throughout the world is massive. We as a family admire his great honesty and loyalty. Whenever he visits us, he shows me great support, care and encouragement. I was honoured when he agreed to write the foreword for my story.

There are not enough words to describe my wonderful friendship with the writer Tahar Ben Jelloun and his lovely family. His children grew up with my children. Tahar was with me and my brother, that dark day in Paris when I was told by Professor Meininger that it was undoubtedly MND. Since then I have always considered him as a big brother. He has stood by me and continues to support me through the toughest times of my life. We have continued to grow closer over the years. We have been through so much together and share so many memories. Again, Tahar has a great sense of humour and laughs a lot. More than that, he has never belittled my hope for the future and always encourages me.

My four children have coped with my illness in different ways as they have grown up. Sawsan, my eldest, was academically bright and a very serious girl. Now she is a grown woman and her timidity sometimes makes her appear cold. In reality, she is sensitive, and tends to suffer in silence. My illness has affected her a lot and she does not like to talk about it. Sabrina is smart and independent. I do not worry about her. She has my energy and the drive for success. She has accompanied me to Paris for my check-ups for several years now. As a result, she understands more about my illness than her siblings, but has remained calm, hopeful and optimistic through the years. Mehdi, my unexpected son, is sensitive about my situation and showers me with hugs and kisses every day. He is a positive boy and tends to be quite carefree, something which sometimes concerns me. Adam, my youngest treasure, has always been especially close to me. Although he looks fit and strong, he is also a deep worrier and I know he is often anxious about me. I am proud of all four of them. They are my greatest achievement.

I know that, given my diagnosis all those years ago, I am lucky that I have had the time granted to me to see my children grow up into adulthood. My children are everything to me and I have done everything I could to raise them the way I wanted and had planned. Watching your children go off into the big, wide, scary world is an experience that every parent must face, but for me it was particularly emotional. Perhaps because I never felt that I had a guarantee that I would see the day. My children have also been my focus – my distraction from my illness – and I was also conscious of losing that.

Raising a family in the shadow of MND

When my two daughters, Sawsan and Sabrina, left for university, I cried a lot but it was oddly easier than letting my son Adam go. Adam decided to go abroad to study in Switzerland. For some reason I could not accept his absence. I did not understand why I could not overcome this sense of great loss. I became so depressed and cried every time I passed his room. Perhaps it was because Adam is my youngest child.

In Switzerland, to begin with Adam started to suffer from homesickness and eventually he was returning home for weekends. A few months later, though, Adam was completely changed. He had been at the Lycée with so many different nationalities and yet he had become more interested in meeting students from Morocco at university and connecting with that part of his heritage. Luckily, he met some of the kindest boys and they finally helped him settle into his studies. They all remain friends today.

My son Mehdi chose to stay in London. I remember asking him if he wanted to follow his brother to study in Switzerland and he immediately answered, "No, Momsie, I want to stay with you." I remember we both burst into tears. At that moment, I just wished that I was able to hug him tight to my chest but my arms would not move. My condition has robbed me of so much.

All four of my children have completed their studies and have graduated from universities with good degrees. Seeing my daughter Sawsan walking across the stage at New York University to receive her third degree – a Masters in International Relations – in 2016 was a monumental moment for me. Sawsan had received her first degree from Durham and her second from the City of London Business School. After graduating, she worked for J.P. Morgan for two years. But her ambition led to further postgraduate study. She then went on to work for Hillary Clinton in her Presidential campaign. Sawsan is a good example of how commitment and hard work pay off. After years of dedication, sacrifice and self-discipline, Sawsan has achieved great success with her studies and career. She held on to her dreams when things were tough. Her achievement is proof that she is strong and unbreakable like her mother. I never thought that I would have lived to see her achieve so much. I am extremely proud of my baby.

My younger daughter Sabrina gained her degree from the University of Warwick, which was also where she met her future husband. She went on to achieve a Masters at Cass Business School in London. Sabrina is not as natural an academic as Sawsan, but manages to combine her competence at studying with a very astute business sense. I have full confidence in Sabrina's ability to survive and flourish.

My two sons took more career orientated degree subjects. Mehdi graduated from Westminster with a degree in marketing. Adam chose to follow our family interests, by taking a degree in International Hospitality Management at the university in Switzerland.

A child's graduation is a big deal for every parent, but even more intense for a terminally ill mother. Every one of my children's graduations has signified something much deeper for me – again, perhaps because I was never certain that I would be here to see the day. Pride and a sense of victory are the two things that I felt in those moments. I felt pride because of what my children had achieved. The fact that I was there to witness their success and achievement also marked a victory for me over my illness. It had taken so much from me but it could not rob me of those precious moments.

Thirty years with MND

After my diagnosis, I continued to see Professor Meininger at his clinic in Paris every two months. Luckily, I had other excellent doctors, who have guided me through my darkest thoughts and encouraged me to stay positive. Both of the doctors who have seen me regarding my condition, Professor Nigel Leigh and Professor Ammar Al-Chalabi, have been very caring. Professor Al-Chalabi is a particularly special person in my life. Throughout my battle with this disease, he has been there at every stage. I sometimes wonder if there are words that could express my gratitude to him. My daughters feel the same about his support. He has skilfully and sensitively kept me up to date with assessments of my condition and with any new breakthroughs in research.

Naima

In the beginning, when my symptoms were slow to progress and my illness did not affect the rhythm of my life, my main fear was of the day when I would lose my independence. I tried hard to banish all negative thoughts from my mind and keep my focus away from that fear. I tried to stay busy. I deliberately engaged myself in as many activities as I could. I kept telling myself that the real race was coming. I thought that I could overcome what was happening to my body by using the power of my mind and positive thoughts. For as long as I could, I did the things I had always done. I did my own shopping and banking. I visited restaurants with my family or friends and I travelled as much as I could. I was determined that my life would go on as it had been for as long as my body allowed.

The knowledge that the illness could change my situation at any time would often bubble to the surface, no matter how busy I kept myself. I found various ways of dealing with my anxiety at those times. In the beginning, I used to find that one remedy for my stress was to drive my car. I loved driving from the moment I arrived in London, but it became something more than a pleasure. Driving was my freedom. In the car, I could go anywhere. It was also my time alone to work through my thoughts. I didn't have to put on a happy face when it was just me behind the wheel. I would drive for hours, sometimes out into the country where I would find myself in places unknown to me. I would lose track of time and have to rush to get back in time to collect my children from school. Music was also a great release for me on these drives. I used to listen to my favourite songs of the sixties: Demis Roussos, the Bee Gees, Cat Stevens. The music of my past took me back to when I was young – before MND. I also loved the sound of Andalous music, especially when I missed my home in Morocco and my dear brothers. My other, quite different, source of solace was listening to the Koran on audio book. The familiar words reminded me of my faith and that everything happens for a reason. This belief soothed me and gave me hope.

The day that I received a letter from the DVLA informing me that I was no longer allowed to drive because of my diagnosis, I was devastated. I was still a more-than-competent driver, and driving had become part of the way I coped with day-to-day life with MND. I was more than competent behind the wheel of a car. It felt like a huge part of my precious independence was being taken away before I was ready to let it go. More than that, being able to drive was key in my being able to care for my children. I did the school runs, dropped them at activities or friends' houses and took them to visits to the doctor. I was, despite everything that was happening to me, still perfectly capable of managing an automatic-drive car. I decided that I wouldn't let them stop me. And so I decided to protest the order.

I called my doctor, Dr. Jeffrey Gawler, and explained to him what had happened. He was sympathetic and promised me that he would try to sort it out. First, he asked me to show him how I handled my car and take him on a drive. I agreed and drove to pick him up. Before he got into the car, jokingly, I advised him to say "Goodbye" to his wife. We both laughed as we set off. I was quietly confident that he would see I was perfectly competent behind the wheel. And happily, he was able to pass my driving ability and wrote to the DVLA accordingly. My licence was not revoked and I was able to continue driving. It was a relief and a rare moment of victory. Honestly, it gave me a new lease of life. When I was driving I felt free again. It allowed me to push the physical difficulties I was experiencing away from my mind for a few hours.

My appearance had always been very important to me. I take care in how I look and how I dress. Before MND took most of my mobility, I liked clothes and fashion and I took care in selecting pieces for my wardrobe. When my illness began to advance, I was determined to hold onto elegance for as long as I could. I wasn't going to write myself off. So I carried on shopping for the best designer clothes that I could afford from my favourite stores. Going to the hairdresser became more than a luxury for me. It was a necessity because it was another investment in myself. I refused to be scared by my uncertain future and took a leap of faith that I had a little bit longer when I decided to have a major makeover of my teeth. It was painful, expensive and took months to complete. But at the time, it focused my mind and body on an improvement for myself, when I knew that the pathway was inevitable decline. It was a valuable diversionary tactic. And I was delighted with the results.

My body eventually started to go through some bad physical changes. I knew that the wasting muscles in my shoulders were changing the shape of my body and I hated that. I did not want anyone to notice these changes and wanted to remain as elegant as I could. So I padded my shoulders every day to hide the changes. The wasting of the muscles in my chin also became noticeable, and that affected the shape of my lips. To disguise this, I used only a light shade of lipstick colour and tried not to close my mouth. My neck also dropped and changed, so I stopped wearing low-cut tops. I adapted every time I noticed a change in my body. It was part of the way I coped with it. I refused to let myself be drawn into the darkness. For me, my chic and classic look was part of who I was. I wasn't going to let my disability define me. Keeping control of the way I looked in whatever way I could for as long as I could gave me powerful and positive feelings.

Indeed, there were times after my diagnosis when my pretence was so successful that it was often difficult for people to see that I was ill. One year, I travelled to Florida with my children to visit Disneyland. By then, I needed the support of Habiba to keep my balance. My brother had explained to the airline in advance that I would need help to go through the gate so the staff were expecting me. I was dressed quite lightly and was wearing make-up as I approached the gate with Habiba holding my arm. A lady from the airline came forward and, to my astonishment, instead of taking my arm she gently pulled Habiba away from me and firmly guided *her* through security. She had assumed that Habiba was the one who needed support. Habiba did not have the English to correct her mistake so was shuffled through the gate, looking back over her shoulder at me standing by myself. Poor Habiba! I must admit that I creased up with laughter, as did my children.

Now my illness is impossible to disguise and so I live life as a visibly disabled person. Everyone knows the saying "Never judge a book by its cover" and, whilst that is good advice, it is not followed by everyone during everyday life. Whilst friends have been supportive and will take the time to listen with care and patience to me when we talk, strangers can sometimes be outright dismissive. People sometimes make presumptions about me and my mental state based on my appearance or the manner of my speech. Anyone with a disability will have had the experience of being unfairly judged by others. When people see someone in a wheelchair, they automatically begin making assumptions about them and about the things they are capable of. Sadly, some see only an external appearance and draw conclusions from that – and it is wrong. Sometimes, when I meet people for the first time, they will assume that I am mentally disabled because of the way I speak. They will often ignore me and speak to the people I am with *about* me, rather than directly *to* me – even though I am present and able to answer for myself. I often I find myself excluded and sometimes quite literally overlooked when I am in my wheelchair. I've learned not to mind too much if this happens with strangers, because they do not know me. However it has upset me more when it has been someone whom I know and who knows my diagnosis.

Naima

One summer, I was in a restaurant for a lunch date with a friend when we encountered an acquaintance. The acquaintance could barely look at me – it was as if I was invisible to him. He spoke only to my friend. I already felt awkward and embarrassed. Then I was shocked when, suddenly, he asked her, "Does Naima understand our conversation?" I tried to ignore this idiotic question and smiled but inside I felt hurt and degraded. Of course I could understand their conversation. There was nothing wrong with my mind. Later, Habiba confessed that she was also disturbed and upset by his behaviour. I am sure he didn't mean to, but his words hurt me deeply. My illness had taken a lot from me but it hadn't taken my power of understanding or the ability to speak for myself. My body might have changed and weakened but my mind was still sharp and quick. How could he think that I was incapable of understanding him? How could he be *so* ignorant?

There is something deeper to us than just the physical shells that we inhabit. Look at Hawking and all that he achieved despite the failings of his physical body. Or F.D. Roosevelt who was one of the most influential American presidents in history, despite being paralysed from the waist down. We are *not* our bodies. And we should not judge or try to define others based on what we *think* we see of them.

Just because my legs and arms don't listen to me does not mean that my life is going to stop. I know that being still here with a nimble and healthy mind is a blessing. I really do not mind the wheelchair or other equipment that facilitates my everyday life. And I know that I am fortunate in having such devoted help so that my life is made more bearable. What is crucial for me is to remain positive and to hang on for as long as possible. I try not to think about what might happen next to my body. I try just to carry on doing what I *can* do until my last breath – no matter what happens. I have learned what I can physically tolerate and what I cannot.

I have a full understanding of the seriousness of my illness and, despite medical advances in MND care and research, I know that there is little hope of finding a cure. But I have found strength to carry on and the courage to fight the illness. I partly found this strength through my Muslim faith.

Even after I revealed my condition to my family, I continued to keep my disease concealed from many of my friends and people in my life. Whilst this was an additional burden to me, I did this for as long as I could. I wanted to make sure that this disease couldn't define me. I wanted to remain Naima and not become "Naima who has MND" – even if it was only in the eyes of others. It was only when I could not walk and began to use a wheelchair that I finally had to break the news of my diagnosis to everyone in my life.

I am lucky that I have a group of amazing close friends who have been incredible in supporting me right from the beginning. They have been a significant factor in giving me the strength to keep fighting. Gerald and Jane – two great friends – not only always knew about my diagnosis and how serious it was, but they understood *why* I needed try to mask the reality from the wider public and they helped me to do that for as long as possible. Every time I see Jane, I forget all my pain. She has a strong personality, is a hard-working mum, and cracks me up with her funny jokes. Gerald takes the pressure off me in a different way. He is patient and doesn't talk to me like a disabled person. I enjoy his insight into history, current affairs and politics. More than this, we both enjoy a good gossip, whether it's about people we know or people we do not.

Social interactions are very good for my mental well-being. And it helps me to focus on something other than my own pain. Being able to talk with other people about their ups and downs is a natural relief and a welcome escape from my own fears and pain. I am lucky in having friends who also have a good sense of humour and are always ready to joke about other people and, most importantly, themselves. Some people find it hard to understand my sense of humour regarding my life and what has happened to my body, but I use humour as a coping mechanism myself so I relate to people who do the same. I have always tried to make the most of my bad situation with laughter.

Living with MND has given me a new perspective on many things. Despite my best efforts, I sometimes become upset and irritated when people complain about what I see as minor problems. Some everyday worries and frustrations honestly now seem stupid to me. I can't fathom wasting energy getting angry about things that are small, inconsequential and out of our control. I wouldn't want to fill my days with negativity when I could choose to look on the bright side. It's easy to take our blessings for granted, to lose perspective and forget how precious everyday things are. I've found that people who are relentlessly negative in their outlook are invariably people who have had relatively easy lives and haven't faced any real problems. Perhaps people who have experienced real adversity have more resilience. Perhaps it's simply that some people are more selfish than others and can't see beyond their own world. All I know is that MND has given me more perspective than I ever thought I would have and, as a result, I have little time for people who want to wallow in self-pity.

Everyone reacts to and deals with terminal illness in a different way. There are those who, perhaps accidentally, belittle me by refusing to see beyond the limits of my body. They see a woman in a wheelchair and seem unable to acknowledge that I still have a quick and active mind. And then there are others that will pity me. I try not to notice the commiseration in people's eyes and their tone of voice when they meet me for the first time. I refuse to accept any feelings of pity for me. I am more than my illness. For my family and my friends, I am the spiritual helper and the listener. I am the one that they come to for advice and guidance. I am the source of positivity and support. And I refuse to pity myself. Throughout all the years I have lived with MND, I have never complained about my condition to anyone. And for as long as I could, I tried to live life as normally as possible and be thankful for every day. My focus has always been on how to live with Motor Neurone Disease, not how to die from it.

Epiphanies

Most Motor Neurone Disease sufferers do not live beyond three years after diagnosis. Somehow – perhaps it is the will of God – I have endured for more than thirty and I am still here. I still have times when I am amazed at the fact that I am alive and that I have survived this long. I have seen my children complete their educations and start their adult lives. For me, this is a real miracle.

My love and determination to remain here as long as possible for my family is what keeps me going, but I would be lying if I said I had not contemplated the end. I often think of the moment when I will have to give up my fight. Many times when I have felt my body failing me, I see death in front of my eyes. Then I immediately picture the faces of my children and I begin to fight and resist again. Tuesday 20th March 2012 was one of those moments. I had a horrible experience which was possibly the closest I have come to death since my diagnosis. Quite suddenly, at five in the morning, my breathing became difficult. My breathing had been normal throughout that night but for some reason I suddenly found myself struggling to take a breath. Panicked, I tried to wake Habiba so she could sit me up to ease access to my airways. It was something we had been trained to do by my physiotherapist. But, unable to take a breath, I found myself unable to make any noise. Frighteningly, my breathing rapidly became much worse and I was still unable to wake Habiba. I felt myself suffocating. In that moment, I thought I might be finally facing the end.

Many MND sufferers have breathing and choking episodes as the disease affects the ability to swallow. I knew of many people with my illness who had suffocated. In that horrible moment, I started to picture my own funeral in my mind. I tried to calm myself to avoid making my situation worse but it felt like I was seconds from death and – honestly – I was scared. I started to sweat and to shake as I fought really hard to regain my breath. Somehow, I managed to make a noise and it was enough to rouse Habiba. She pulled me upright, calling for help. My children and my brother Abdeslam, who happened to be staying in London for a couple of days, rushed into my bedroom in a panic.

As I felt loved ones around me, I was still fighting for breath and waiting for the storm to pass. I realised then that my deepest fear wasn't death – it was dying *there* in front of my family. I was terrified that I was going to die in front of my children and my dear brother. My brother and I are the same person, with two different bodies, but one mind. I knew that seeing the moment I died would destroy him. And my children? I couldn't let them witness my death. That realisation and having all the people I loved around me suddenly gave me an incredible strength. As I fought to regain my breath, I was praying to God to give me

Epiphanies

more time. God must have been listening because I started to recover and my breath came slowly back to me. I gulped in oxygen as my family comforted me. It took a full thirty minutes for my breathing to return to normal and several weeks to recover entirely from the episode. Afterwards I temporarily lost use of my voice. And I suffered terrible spasms of coughing and was drained of energy for some time. But I had survived. It was another real miracle.

I had contemplated my death before, but this frightening experience changed me. It not only strengthened my resolve to appreciate every minute of my life, it made me re-evaluate some things in my life. It woke me up and made me think about things in a different way. The issue that was mostly on my mind at that point was my daughter's future. At university, Sabrina had met a young man called Eugeny. They had fallen in love and she had been devoted to him for seven years. I had raised my children to be independently minded but I was very set on what *I* believed was best for them. Eugeny, the man my daughter had fallen in love with, was from a different country and culture to our family, and when Sabrina raised the prospect of them marrying, I was reluctant to give my blessing. Our background is one of close-knit communities and family ties. What if a new husband took her away from our orbit, from her cultural heritage and her family? For some time, I had been strongly resisting any suggestion of Sabrina marrying Eugeny, even though I saw my daughter suffer increasing unhappiness because of my position.

My close brush with death that night changed all that. I realised that my reservations and fears should not dominate my daughter's decisions and that her happiness was paramount. Sabrina was a highly independent, thoughtful and mature young woman, who knew what she was doing. She and Eugeny had a strong and good relationship, despite all my worries about the differences between their backgrounds and cultures. The experience of coming so

Naima

close to death made me realise that I had to change the way I saw things. I needed to move out of my restricted ways of thinking. People should not be measured by their nationalities or cultures. They should be measured by their actions, their thoughts and their character. This is what I came to realise in the days after that terrifying night. I decided to free myself of the antiquated thoughts that I had been attached to for too long. Eugeny was a good man. He loved my daughter and I knew that he would take care of her. I understood that Sabrina must follow her destiny. I told her that I would give my blessing to her marriage.

My decision transformed Sabrina's life. She is a loyal and loving daughter and so she had been torn between her duty to me and her desire to build her own life. Now she had my blessing to marry the man she loved and the man *she* had chosen to share her life with. Released from my old thinking, I looked forward to her wedding and to what I hoped would be many years of happy marriage for my daughter.

Sabrina had a wonderful wedding to Eugeny. I was delighted to be involved in the organising of a wedding which I had never thought that I would live to see. It was the most beautiful wedding with a fusion of traditional Moroccan and contemporary European, uniting their two different cultures in the harmony of love. I helped Sabrina to choose all the Moroccan traditional kaftans for the ceremony. I even had a hand in choosing the menu and selecting her hairdresser and make-up artist. Friends and family gathered from all over the world in a magnificent marquee filled with flowers and music. After the ceremony, the guests danced until dawn. I was overwhelmed with joy and pride. I am happy that, out of one of the worst experiences of my life, I was able to grow as a person and that a new happiness was born.

Epiphanies

Sadly, in February 2015, my beloved mother died. In the weeks preceding, she had become weaker and seemed to have an awareness that she was reaching of the end of her life. We were all with her at her passing, and she slipped away, peacefully, in her sleep. I'm sure that it would be everybody's choice to have such an ending. As her baby girl – which I always will be – it was what I wished for her. And it is what I wish for myself but, unfortunately, I cannot be optimistic that my passing will be as peaceful. My mother was a big part of our family. And she not only had a good death but she had a good life. I consider her lucky in terms of her health, especially in her later years. She never suffered any major illness and was blessed with an amazing family, who looked after her until her last moments. And I am grateful for that. Nevertheless, I didn't anticipate that my mother's death would affect me so deeply. When she passed, it took a part of me away.

Later in the same year, there was a much happier event: the wedding of my eldest child, Sawsan, to her boyfriend Mehdi. The two had known each other as teenagers and had encountered each other again when they both found themselves in Washington. The idea that I would be able to see *any* of my children get married had felt like a dream since I was diagnosed. Now I would be at my other daughter's wedding.

Despite my joy at the news, I admit that my old feelings of reluctance came up again and I felt unprepared to give my beloved daughter away. I chided myself. Was it not just yesterday that I had received my sentence of death? I was lucky just to be here to witness my little girl marry the man she loved. My conflicting feelings gave me a terrible temper and powerful headaches in the months before the wedding. Fortunately, I overcame my discomfort and I was able to have the same involvement as with Sabrina's wedding. The wedding was extremely beautiful. As my children were born and raised in London, they are very attached to British customs, but they also have strong bonds with their traditional heritage in Morocco, and this was reflected in the wedding ceremony.

There was a moment of intense emotion, when Sawsan rose and proposed a toast. Slowly, my daughter addressed me:

> *Mum, I love you. You are what keeps me going every day. Thank you for your unconditional love, for always believing in me and for your unparalleled courage.*
>
> *I think I speak for everyone here when I say you are the strongest and bravest woman I know, and a real inspiration to not only the millions of people around the world living with ALS but to every single person who has ever felt desperate, defeated and like they wanted to give up. Thank you for making me the fighter I am today.*
>
> *And my two uncles who like to go unnoticed, but not tonight, sorry! This is as much your night as it is mine.*
>
> *You are both the glue that keeps our family together. Thank you for always putting us first, for working so hard and for giving up so much so that we can have so much more.*

I felt elated that I had been an inspiration to her during my years of struggle with MND, and I loved her for the special mention of her uncles who had given so much of themselves to help our family. In the midst of all the celebrations, both Sawsan and I cried tears of happiness.

Epiphanies

In 2019, there was another unexpected turn of events in my life and the lives of my family. My ex-husband and I had been divorced for some years by then. He had remarried – a younger woman – and I felt that he had made a new life for himself and that I would never see him again. The pain that he had caused me during our marriage, when he abandoned our family, and during our divorce, was still there, but I had moved on. I grew up in a loving Muslim family, where we never kept grudges or harboured resentments. My illness also played a big part in how I view these things. Life is too short to hold on to hatred. You can't change the past or fix other people's mistakes so hanging on to grudges will never make anyone feel better. But those views of mine were about to withstand a test.

One evening in Tangier, I was on my computer. Abdeslam was with me, watching the television. Adam came into the room and I noticed that he was very stressed. I could see something was worrying him.

I asked him, "What's wrong, my son?"

He replied in a sad tone, "I had a call from someone. They told me that my dad has cancer and he is seriously ill in London. He seems to be all alone."

I felt numb and shocked. I remained silent for a few seconds. Then I heard Abdeslam say quietly to my son, "What goes around comes around. I don't think we really care about what happens to him." My brother had never forgiven my husband for abandoning me and his family or for the animosity he showed during our divorce.

But, in that moment, I could see the real concern on my son's face and I felt my own anger and hurt regarding my ex-husband fade to the background. I knew that it was up to me to make a decision. I said to my brother, "He is his father and it's Adam's duty to take care of him if he is sick – no matter what."

Adam looked surprised by my reaction but, at the same time, I could see he was relieved.

"You must contact him," I told my son. "Contact your father. If he needs help we must offer it to him."

Adam took a deep breath, looked at me, and said, "Are you sure, Momsie?"

I thought about it again for a moment. But I knew what I had to do.

"If we offer help for him that does not mean that I excuse his terrible past behaviour. It's for my own peace of mind that I choose to try to forgive him. I just want to release my painful feelings of the past and for you to repair your broken relationship with him. Holding on to the pain will not solve anything. And if he is sick, we need to help him."

I knew, for sure, that many people in my life would not agree with or understand my decision. Many of my friends thought I was mad for accepting him back into my life after everything he had put me through. Many would find forgiving someone who has hurt you and deserted you – let alone at a time when you were seriously ill – simply impossible. But I knew I was doing the right thing and I thanked God for giving me a heart that is capable of forgiveness. It meant I could tell my son what he needed to hear. He needed to go to his father.

Adam and Sawsan called Sabrina, who was in London, and asked her to find out more about the situation with their father. A few days later she called us, and I remember Sabrina almost screaming on the phone in distress at what she'd found. Her father had been sleeping on the floor at his nephew's small flat. He was in a terrible state and was looking very thin and miserable. It appeared that his new wife was not actively involved in looking after him now he was sick. And he had nowhere else to live. When I learned this, I could not help but remember his own treatment of me when I became ill. Sabrina had also learned that his cancer was very advanced. He was dying. His time was running out.

Epiphanies

I suggested to Sabrina that she should initially move him to our family home in London and out of the tiny flat. There, he would be more comfortable and we could organise proper care for him. Once there, he was joined by his children, who he reconnected with. His daughters began taking him to the hospital appointments for his treatment. They fed him and nursed him. Adam also visited and helped care for his father. The man that I thought was gone from my life forever was back in our home.

Many have told me that I am to be admired for my forgiveness of the man who had caused me so much distress. I am always quick to state that it was not an easy decision for me to make and it was definitely not an easy time for me. The reality is that this period took a great psychological toll on me. It *hurt* to try to forgive him. It took a great deal of my mental strength to do what I knew to be right and invite him back into our home. I was still in Tangier when I heard that he had asked to see me. Very reluctantly, and for the sake of my children, I agreed. I went back to London and prepared myself for the reunion. It had been almost twenty years since he left us, but when I saw him for the first time after our divorce, all the past came back to me. I felt the anger, the hurt and the sadness I'd experienced as a result of everything that had happened between us. It was a feat to let go of those very real emotions and focus on the present and what was happening to him.

The next few months, as his cancer progressed, continued to be emotionally challenging for me. My children were desperate to make the most of the time to be with him after so many years without their father. They were pleased that he was back in their lives and their joy made me happy. I was proud of how my children handled the situation. They had endured years of his absence but they still found the strength and love to care for him in his last days. Sabrina and Sawsan took turns in cleaning and changing him, as his condition worsened. They researched any medications that could prolong his life for a few more months.

As his condition declined, he had a kind of transformation and began to express a lot of sadness and regret. It seemed that, as he drew closer to death, he was revisiting some of the choices he had made in life. In the end, I found that he needed my forgiveness as much as I needed the strength to give it to him. We travelled to Tangier before his condition became too bad to travel. There, he and I were sat with some of my old friends enjoying a lunch at one of my favourite cafes. The cafe is just outside Tangier and there is a beautiful view across the mountains and forests. There, surrounded by friends, the father of my children, and the man who had caused me so much pain, took my hand. He was very sick at this point. I looked at him and saw that he was full of emotion.

"Forgive me," he said, and he kissed my hand gently. "I am so sorry about the past."

I felt the weight of the moment and when I looked around, I saw that all my friends were moved to tears. Perhaps it was because he now had his own experience of a life-altering disease, or perhaps it was because he could see his own death, that had caused him to have this moment of reflection. It was a day that I will always remember.

We established that immunotherapy treatment was the only thing that could help him and they arranged for several sessions. But he reacted very badly to it and therefore it had to be stopped. From then on, the treatment he received was palliative. To manage the pain, he was frequently given a high dose of morphine intravenously by the nurse, who was always with him. But his condition declined rapidly to the point that he stopped eating and was put on a drip. Despite everything, he remained lucid throughout.

Epiphanies

In his final days, it was extremely hard for me to watch my ex-husband endure terrible pain every day and to know that there was nothing anyone could do to help. The only thing we could do for him was just be there. I wanted to show that I was the sort of person that, no matter what, would never turn my back on anyone in need of my help and support. But it remained a very difficult time for me. I was caught in a living hell. I struggled to encourage him to stay positive and fight on. When we talked, I sensed that he became calmer, happier and a little more optimistic. Perhaps because I had lived with my own painful condition for so long, I was able to show him how to find the strength within himself and face what was coming. Eventually, all the old painful memories vanished from my mind, and I became more focused on helping him mentally. All the details of his stay in our family home as his life ended are engraved on my mind forever, in a way that no words can explain. I shall always be haunted by the painful memories of his terrible state before he passed away. His cancer treatment was extremely aggressive, and the side effects were horrible.

In those final months of his life, I learned that the twists and turns of our lives can bring us to extraordinary moments. In a strange way his terrible illness eased away some of the bitterness of our divorce from my memories. And it reunited my children with their father. I am grateful that they had this chance to reconcile with him before he died. My ex-husband stayed with us for a year whilst the cancer ate away at him. He passed away in Tangier in 2021. I don't know if I've achieved forgiveness but I understand that it is complicated and you have to work hard at it. And it is always better than hanging on to hate and resentment.

Naima

The most wonderful blessings that I never imagined I would live to see were the births of my grandchildren. Sabrina and Eugeny welcomed Sofia and Rayan. Sawsan and Mehdi later brought Ali and Salma into our family. From the moments these four beautiful souls were born they had my whole heart. I treat all my four grandchildren equally and love each one to bits. Even so, somehow, my relationship with Sofia – my first grandchild and my treasure – has always been something quite special. My grandchildren have never known me without MND, and Sofia has always seen beyond the disease to the real me. And she led the way for her brother and cousins in that. For the first three years of her life I was mostly the one who cared for her every day. I thought of myself as her guardian angel, always there in any difficulty. Even through her school days as she got older, we have remained close and happy to be together.

We have a special bond. From the day she was born, she has often slept in the same room and sometimes in the same bed with me. We have family photographs of us both fast asleep. I am wearing my breathing equipment and Sofia is often nestled up against me, her arms and legs tumbling over her sleeping grandmother. Even when she started to grow up, she still often asked to sleep in my room with me and her baby cousin, Salma. I was able to look after Sofia when she was very small and, happily, I was able to do the same for Salma, my youngest grandchild. These days, Habiba is often caring for all of us and I joke that we are like an odd little nursery as I need as much care as the babies. I think there is a strong connection between myself and my grandchildren because of this time we spend together. Sometimes, when we are all gathered in the living room as a family, I will be the first to hear the sounds that tell me that Salma has stirred from her slumber in the next room.

I never imagined how much love my granddaughters Sofia and Salma would bring me. They are both very special in every way. Rayan and Ali give me joy in a different way. Rayan is very adventurous, whilst Ali is more cautious in his approach to things. It is fascinating to see their different characters. And there is the added joy of seeing my grandchildren learn to play with one another.

My beloved grandchildren always lift me up whenever I feel down. When I am with them, my attention is solely concentrated on them. The four of them are a joy that takes me out of myself and makes me forget my pain. The love I feel for them has made me want to fight to stay with them more than ever. When we go out together, Sofia and Salma will quarrel over who should sit on my lap in the wheelchair. Having them in my life really compensates for what has been robbed from me. But what is sometimes tough to bear is that I cannot reach out and hold my baby grandchildren. I can't hug them or play with them. I long to do these things. Not being able to do these things – these very human acts of love – gives me a great deal of emotional and psychological pain. It is another joy that my disease has taken from me. Yet the mere presence of Sofia, Rayan, Ali and Salma in my life – with their beautiful, innocent, smiling faces – inspires me and strengthens my determination to fight. I want them to have good and happy memories of me more than anything. There is nothing more special in the world than being a grandma and I am grateful I have had the chance. It is something that I never imagined I would be.

Pandemic

It's a human conceit to be certain that we will have time for things we want to do. "I'll do it tomorrow or even next year," we say, with the confidence that we will *have* tomorrow and that we will *have* next year. And if we question this certainty, we might see that it's not as solid as we imagine it to be. So we often avoid doing that. It's one of the many ways of navigating through life that humans have. We don't like to contemplate that our time here is limited. One of the things that a terminal illness like MND strips from sufferers is that certainty. Suddenly the realisation that we might not have a "next year" or even a "tomorrow" becomes something that colours all our moments. All our plans become more urgent with the loss of that certainty.

In December 2019, the world watched in horror as a mysterious virus erupted from a small province in China. The virus was killing people. Within months the virus – named Covid-19 – had spread to every corner of the globe and was a threat to the health of the entire planet. Governments responded with restrictions on social mixing. Lockdowns were called in almost all countries and people were asked to stay in their homes and avoid mixing with anyone outside of their household to help stave off the spread of the deadly virus. It was a time of great uncertainty and worry for everyone. The virus was vicious and, although many pulled through, nobody had any way of knowing whether it might prove fatal for them or at least lead to life-changing after-effects.

In many ways, Covid-19 was a great leveller. It was a threat to the health of the entire human race. For those frightening months and years, almost everyone had certainty stripped away from them. We didn't know if or when a vaccine would be developed or whether a cure might be found. And nobody had any certainty that anything would ever be the same again. For many, it meant reassessing their ideas of community and the value they placed on every life. Many made sacrifices for others, even strangers, in a way that they just hadn't before. I hoped that those insights into a world of more compassion and empathy wouldn't be lost as the world returned to something like normal.

In many ways, lockdown was a window into the world of people who live with a terminal illness. The diagnosis of terminal illness is, in itself, a sentence of isolation. And the virus was also a uniquely dangerous threat to anyone living with underlying health conditions. During the days of the lockdowns, I couldn't help but contemplate the added hardship it imposed on all of us Motor Neurone Disease sufferers. We all want to be alone from time to time and, if we are lucky to have a lovely home, it is not such a burden to stay there. But prolonged social isolation is terribly harmful, especially

Pandemic

for people such as myself. For terminally ill people like me, the added loneliness and isolation that came with the pandemic lockdowns was toxic.

My own experience of lockdown was miserable. I grew exhausted from trying to stay my usual calm and positive self when it felt like everything was working against me. The difficulties of fighting MND – of being wheelchair-bound and of having to rely on Habiba for everything – are things that can drain me of strength during normal times. The added threat of Covid-19 to my health, along with the crushing isolation of having to be separated from the rest of the world and those I loved the most, made this struggle so much harder. I found that I really wanted to converse with someone outside our little bubble – with *anyone*. It is something that is hard to explain but I found myself becoming extremely stressed – much more than normal. It was almost as though my brain was in overload.

Before the lockdowns, my grandchildren would come from school every day to have their supper with me and talk about their day. They would fill me in on the ups and downs and stories of school life. Their presence was a bright spot in my days. Being around my children and grandchildren has always taken my focus off my own struggles. I feel energised around them. However, during lockdown they were not able to come and visit me. I felt cut off from their lives and I missed their laughter and vitality. I felt I lost something of a lifeline without the childish energy they brought to my days. I felt drained. My children would bring them by the house on their daily walks but, like many grandparents, I could only see them through my window. It broke my heart.

There is a kind of imprisonment that my illness imposes but lockdowns brought a new one and I know this is something that many others will have experienced. I also felt the pressure of my clock ticking even more during those dark times of isolation. The months of 2020 creaked by as the world haltingly staggered back into some sort of action. Every month that the world held its breath in lockdown was a month I was losing from the time I had left. I felt like I was having time stolen from me, and it was such a precious thing for me. A year is not the same for everyone. For people like me, with life-limiting illness, we need to make the most of the time we have left and every month – every day – that I waited for my world to open up again was agonising.

I think the pandemic gave many people a chance to understand others – especially those less fortunate than themselves. Perhaps it was because people had the time to sit and recognise realities that aren't the same as theirs. Questions were asked about support for people with underlying health conditions that hadn't really been addressed before. Inequalities in both wealth and health were exposed. For me, that can only be a good thing and I hope that we don't lose sight of these issues in our society now that we have taken the sting out of Covid-19. I hope that we continue, as a society, to recognise the needs of others and try to make our world more inclusive and inviting for people with disabilities or health issues. If the pandemic taught us anything, it has to be that we don't exist in a vacuum – we are a community and we must care for each other.

I had few bright spots during the days of lockdown but one was remote contact with my family. I would video call with my brother Ahmed regularly. He would always try to make me laugh, with his funny jokes and offbeat sense of humour. We spent hours on the phone talking and gossiping with one another during those days. His presence – even if just on the phone or on screen – was a great comfort to me.

In September 2020, I hadn't heard from Ahmed for some days and so I was pleased to receive a call from him one Saturday. He was in a positive mood and I was grateful to hear his voice. What he didn't tell me during that call, and what I didn't for a moment

Pandemic

suspect, was that Ahmed had contracted Covid-19. He and the rest of my family had decided to hide this from me. They did not want to worry me. Ahmed was being taken care of by His Majesty, King Mohammed VI, who had arranged for him to be taken to the military hospital in Rabat. After several days of treatment, he began to show signs of recovery and it looked like he might soon be able to leave hospital. The Saturday he called me, he was still in the hospital but I had no idea.

Something must have triggered my instincts, though, because, after that call, I had a feeling that something was not right. I was so convinced that something was wrong that, later that night, I tried to call him again, but his phone was switched off. I called Abdeslam and asked him if everything was okay. I told him I was worried about our brother. Abdeslam, worried about my health and mental strength, tried to assure me and calm me down but still didn't reveal the truth to me. Everything in me screamed that something was wrong. I called Adam and insisted that he tell me what was happening. Adam could hear my distress at the idea that something was being hidden from me. And so he told me the truth. He told me that Ahmed was in hospital with a chest infection caused by Covid-19 but that he was recovering. I was shocked and naturally worried – this virus was deadly. My brother had been so careful and made many efforts to avoid catching the virus. How on earth could this have happened?

I decided that I had to go home to Tangier to be closer to my brother. My family, realising that I would not be persuaded to stay, arranged for my flight. During my travels, I prayed for my brother's recovery. After we arrived, I tried contacting Abdeslam to ask him whether Ahmed might be discharged from hospital soon. He didn't answer his phone. Again, I knew instinctively that something was terribly wrong. I understood that my family were only trying to protect me, but it was like a nightmare with nobody telling me anything. I became very anxious.

Naima

Eventually, I met up with my family and I knew immediately that something dreadful had happened. My brother and my children broke the news to me. Ahmed's recovery had stalled. He had taken a turn for the worse. Despite the best of care, the virus had taken him away. My brother – my wonderful brother – had died in the military hospital. Ahmed was now one of the many people who were lost to Covid-19.

The grief shattered me. It had truly never occurred to me that I might lose either of my brothers. After my diagnosis, I always expected to be the one to leave them behind. How could Ahmed be gone? I broke down – completely unable to speak. I was numb with shock and with grief. I did not say a word for two days. I just couldn't believe what had happened. I had my entire family around me to support me, but I could do nothing apart from retreat into my sorrow. Three days later, I exploded into uncontrollable tears and fury. I was sad and angry that this awful virus had not just stolen all that time from me but had now taken something far more precious – it had taken my beloved brother.

In my grief, I felt like dying myself, so that I could join my brother. I had truly never known life without Ahmed. When we were young we were both quite happy-go-lucky characters and we had fun together. After my diagnosis, our relationship had changed. From that moment, it was as though everything that Ahmed did, in his work and in life – everything that he achieved – was somehow driven by his desire to take care of me. He had an amazing ability to manage any conflict and tension with humour. He was always laughing and eager to cheer me up when I was down, but beneath all that, he had a deep concern for me and did everything he could to ease my days. Ahmed never grew old – he was always young in spirit.

Because of the loss of him, I now have an emptiness in my heart. Throughout my whole life I have heard people say that time heals all wounds, but that is simply untrue. I will never get over the loss of my brother and I know for sure that my life is irrevocably changed without him. Part of me went with him when he left and what is left of me is in constant terrible pain at his absence. I long to speak to him one last time and say, "Ahmed, there is not a day that I do not cry for you. Yet I know that every day you are with me. I talk to you and tell you everything that is going on in our family. The day you left was Adam's birthday, so I will never be able to celebrate it the same way again. You were the light of our lives. You were my rock, my everything, and uniquely one of a kind. I miss you deeply. I wish I could tell you this. Do not worry. I promised you from the beginning that I would look after our Mehdi for as long as I live. I will carry on doing so until the last breath of my life."

In those dark days following my brother's death, our family was grateful for the kindness shown to us by our community in Tangier. In particular, there are no words to express the gratitude and appreciation of my family to our beloved King Mohammed VI. His Majesty's kindness and sympathy around that time will never be forgotten.

As I write this in 2024, I still have not been able to visit my brother's final resting place. Of everything that Covid-19 took from me, his loss is the one that hurts the most.

Now

Being diagnosed with a terminal illness like Motor Neurone Disease is like moving into an anteroom – a place somewhere between life and death. I have lived every day since my diagnosis wondering if it might be my last. Losing my brother affected me profoundly because I never expected that I would remain in a world where he was not, and so I had not prepared for his loss. I felt a similar loss when my old friend Mary – the first friend I found in London as a young mother – passed away in late 2023. Mary had been a constant in my life. She was not only a fierce friend but Mary *always* made me laugh. She was an absolute force of nature. Her death left me speechless with grief. It was as if a light had switched off in my world. I miss her every day. Losing loved ones when living with a terminal disease is a unique pain.

Naima

Mehdi's wedding was an occasion where – alongside the joy of watching my son marry the woman he loved – I felt that pain so strongly. And I know that Abdeslam felt it too that day because our dear brother, Mehdi's father, should have been there. Both of us wanted to make sure that Ahmed's son had the most wonderful wedding, and so the planning was meticulous. We held the reception in the gardens of our family villa. The entire event was a masterclass in elegance. We had music performed by beautifully dressed musicians who, accompanied by dancers, played Moroccan wedding music as well as English, American and French pop classics. Like my daughters' weddings, the event was a perfect blend of our family's unique heritage and culture. Guests sipped champagne at tables decorated with flowers and flickering candles as my daughters stood to make a toast they had prepared together.

My daughters stood to make a speech. Sawsan was emotional as she revealed to the gathering that she had felt sad – almost angry – as we began to plan this beautiful celebration because we were having to do so without her dear uncle Ahmed. Her emotion, like my own, was triggered by the sense that Ahmed's loss simply wasn't fair. "But I was wrong to feel that way," she said.

> *Because this celebration is exactly what he would have wanted us to do for his son, who meant the world to him. And because I know – and many here will agree with me – that he is here tonight. I feel my uncle in each and every one of you here. My mother has been living with immense guilt since her brother passed away. Living with a terminal illness, she never dreamt she would outlive her brother. But I want to tell you, Mum: it's okay. Mehdi is so blessed to have you – we all are. And you can rest assured that your beloved brother was*

Now

> *in awe of everything you have done for his beloved son, and full of admiration for your courage. So tonight we don't just celebrate the union of two people in love but we also celebrate the unbreakable union of my mother and her two brothers.*

I was struck by her words. Ahmed's death had hit me very hard because of the unique bond I'd shared with my brothers. In a way, my diagnosis and my struggle with this disease had only strengthened the bond that the three of us shared. It had brought us closer together. But what I had felt over Ahmed's death wasn't just loss but also a sense of guilt. *I* was the one with the terminal disease. *I* was the one who had sat in front of a doctor all those years ago as he told me I had just a few years left with my family. And yet I was here to see Mehdi get married and my beloved brother – his father – was not. It wasn't fair.

I sat with tears running down my face. Sabrina, chuckling, announced that Sofia had insisted that she be the one to read her mother's part of the speech. My granddaughter, smiling into the microphone she held in her hands, shyly read from her mother's paper as Sabrina helped her with the bigger words. She thanked everyone for coming. Sabrina then raised a toast to me and my brothers. "Let's raise a toast to my superhero mum, our uncle Abdeslam and our angel-uncle Ahmed." Mehdi and his bride came to greet me with kisses as the guests raised the toast. And in that moment, with Mehdi in front of me, I felt the years fall away and I could see my brother again and I knew that Ahmed was beside me still and that he was with us all on that night.

Sadly, after his wonderful wedding and the high hopes that Abdeslam and I had had for a lasting and happy marriage for Mehdi and his wife, it was a sudden shock to learn that the relationship had broken down. Mehdi came to tell me that things could not carry on and he and his wife were ending their relationship. I was broken-hearted. And worried for my son. But Mehdi will always have the love of me and his family. He will find happiness again somewhere and I know Ahmed will be looking down on him.

In my childhood, I had a premonition that I was not put on earth to be happy and I accepted that I would suffer. For centuries, people have struggled to answer the question of why terrible things happen – especially when they happen to people who haven't done anything to deserve them. Good things don't always happen to good people. There seems to be no reason or fairness to that in the great scheme of life. But for people with faith, like me, there is always hope. Because I believe that everything happens for a reason. Although, in my darkest times, I sometimes felt that God was testing the strength of my belief. And so I have always managed to look for and find joy. Although I never contemplated facing such adversity, I strongly believe that there is a purpose behind the bad things that happen to us. And so my faith has given me the strength to accept what has been dealt to me and to resist being defined by my illness. It gave me the patience and the power to resist despair and to show Him how much trust I have in Him.

It has been more than thirty years since I received the diagnosis that changed my world forever. I think back to the day I first heard the words "Motor Neurone Disease" and then drove to collect my children. I remember that moment where I saw my children waiting outside the school for me. And I remember the quiet promise I made to myself in that instant: that I would fight to see them safely grown up. That dream came true, thanks to God. My children are now all adults with their own wonderful lives. They are well-educated and they have their own brilliant careers. Some of them have started their own families, bringing the joy of grandchildren into my life – something I never dared to dream would happen.

Now

Raising children is not easy, even in the best of circumstances, so when I think about the challenges I've met as a mother, I do feel proud of myself. Seeing my children grow and become wonderful people has made me believe that behind almost any successful and happy person is a loving parent who will do anything for them.

There is a lot of uncertainty in my life. I live each day with the fear of what the future holds. I am not afraid of dying, but I am really terrified of the end stages of MND. This monster disease eventually paralyses almost all the voluntary muscles that allow us to function as humans. There will come a time when every part of my body will have stopped listening to my brain. In my quiet moments, I cannot help but contemplate the moment when I am entirely without movement and perhaps reliant on machines to help me breathe and eat. I am not prepared for this – and perhaps it is true that nobody can ever prepare for that. I do not want to become a "dead living body".

I am also afraid of being a burden to my family. My condition has already affected their lives severely and in different ways. A terminal illness diagnosis is not only a profoundly changing experience for the person suffering from the disease, it also affects their family and loved ones. With MND, they have to watch their loved one battle with possibly one of the cruellest diseases on earth. There is nothing they can do to stop it or to help ease the symptoms. The disease marches on to the inevitable end. Every day I see how desperate and scared my family is for me and, although we rarely talk about it, I know they also think about the day they will lose me. And so I try hard every day to hide my fears beneath the surface of my sea. My smile almost never leaves my face and I laugh and joke. I try to appear brave. I try to hide some of my pain in order to lessen their pain.

So, in many ways, my life is like a show. Friends tell me that I am courageous but I don't feel that I am. I didn't choose to

Naima

face this. Of course I am scared of what my future will bring. How could I not feel frightened? I smile and I laugh when I am around people and they marvel at my "spirit". But of course I have moments of despair. How can I not when I have gone from being a fit and healthy woman to someone trapped in a wheelchair, unable to walk, to speak clearly, and holding the knowledge that this disease will eventually take my life. Often, I cry myself to sleep in the dark. I'm not courageous. No more than anybody else. I appear brave because nobody sees the entirety of my struggle beneath the surface. I still continue, even now, to hide my struggles whenever I can.

Of course, there are moments when I feel pity for myself. In my darker hours, I become fixated on the sadness and frustration I feel at the fact that I have I been robbed of my freedom. I am a prisoner to my illness. In these times, I can see why death might be preferable instead. But I pull myself out of that darkness every time. Each morning, I shed a few tears for myself, before anyone sees me. Then I brush them away from the pillow and I say to myself, "Now, Naima, forward! Fight. Be positive. Do not give up!" I will not let what has been taken from me by MND define me, my life or my family. Life is not fair, but it *is* precious. There is no miracle cure for me or even a realistic hope of one at the moment, but for now, I am still in control of some parts of my damaged body. I have learned to live in the present and be entirely engaged in the moment. Whatever time is left for me, I will use in the best way that I can. I believe in focusing on living and not dying.

Yes, I cry sometimes. But I still laugh often, too. Friends have described my sense of humour as "wicked". I love to laugh. And laughter has often helped me to cope with the devastation of Motor Neurone Disease. Laughter dissolves my fear when it comes upon me and it distracts me when I feel pain. Some people find it hard to understand my sense of humour about my condition. Laughter was and is still my way to deal with my struggle. I believe that laughter helps you stay mentally healthy and makes you feel good. Mehdi and I find much humour in my strange condition. He plays with my fluffy, floppy arms, crossing them and locking them across me, and he has me laughing for hours when he imitates my slurred speech. We both laugh a lot every single day we are together. Sabrina, on the other hand, really hates all of that and becomes upset with our jokes. She does not find it at all funny. But she also understands that laughing at myself and at my circumstances is an important part of my coping mechanisms and she understands it's the way both Mehdi and I deal with what is happening to me.

It's not only been my humour and determination that have kept me going, it is also the wonderful love and support I get from my family. With an eye on an uncertain future, I try and make every moment we are together into a good memory. To be surrounded by family and friends is a joy and gives me much strength.

I love company but there is also a joy in solitude. It is also good to have a few moments alone for quiet thought and contemplation. People fear being lonely but being alone is something that we can take for granted. I am now not able to be alone. There is a risk that I will choke or get into other difficulties if I am ever alone at any moment. So there is always someone – usually Habiba – beside me. I know now that I can never have the experience of being entirely alone again. Solitude is another thing that MND has taken from me. Whilst my gratitude to have my family and friends around me is great, I miss terribly being alone even just for a moment.

My life, before my diagnosis, was very active, but my routine has changed as the disease has taken its course. When I was focused on raising my children, I remained as active as I could. My days were spent driving my children, interacting with other mothers and teachers, organising our home and meals, and helping the children with their studies. Now, my children are all grown up and my days are much quieter. I realise that I kind of miss having my "mum's routine". These days, I do not have to wake up at a particular time for the school run – my schedule has become my own and it has changed again. My days now are simpler.

Every morning, after having my breakfast, I check the news online and reply to any messages and emails. With adaptive technology, I am in touch with friends and keep myself educated on everything going on around the world. I read books and I enjoy escaping into other stories different to my own. Usually, I have an hour of massage and physiotherapy each morning. Lunch is a very important part of the day when all the family gathers for the meal. Lunch is my main meal of the day as I eat lightly in the evening. I still have the ability to swallow and I very much enjoy my food. I am lucky in being still able to eat what I want and I am aware that this might not be forever as my disease progresses. I love our traditional Moroccan dishes – fish tagines, vegetables and fruit. I eat as much organic food as possible. Despite my physical restrictions, I am very actively involved in supervising the care of my beloved grandchildren and they are often in my home whilst their parents are at work. I love that I am still surrounded by children.

Many things have been taken from me by MND. When I think of where I believed I would be when I was first told my diagnosis, I am incredibly thankful to God that I am doing much better than I had ever imagined. It has been a source of immense sadness to watch other sufferers deteriorate at a much faster rate than me, and so I always try to remember how lucky I have been. For a long time, the toll the disease took on my body was almost tolerable and I was able to find ways to manage it. It is a blessing that my condition was relatively

Now

stable for more than twenty years, giving me the time to see my children grow and even to welcome my grandchildren into the world.

Today, despite everything, my life is still amazing and precious to me. I am still just able to use my voice. I sometimes struggle to make myself understood but, with patience and time, I can still converse with my friends and family. It worries me deeply that one day my voice might be silenced. I cannot imagine myself trapped without a voice, unable to express myself or to tell jokes to my son Mehdi. I feel that my voice is my identity and it's part of my personality. It is the thing I fear most losing to Motor Neurone Disease. Today, I am grateful that I can still talk to my grandchildren and tell them stories. I often wonder what will happen if or when I lose my voice. What if I have to talk through a computer? I sometimes imagine, if that were to happen, what I would say to my grandchildren. How would I explain it? Would they understand that the words were still mine? Would they become scared of their dear grandma if her voice was replaced by an electronic one? Would it affect them emotionally to hear a voice that was not their grandma's? That would be one of the hardest things for me to accept and so I try not to think about this possibility.

I fought hard for the right to drive my car for as long as possible but that time has now passed, too. I miss driving so much, but still love to be driven. When we visit Tangier I have a driver, Mohamed, who will take me around town to the spots I remember being as a young girl, when the city was our holiday place. We will drive past the Pasio and I will remember sitting there with my mother and watching the young, fashionable people of Tangier walk by. I will remember the places where I spent my youth with my dear brothers. And I remember Ahmed. My driver in the city has been shuttling me around for so long now that he knows where I want to go just by listening to the quietest of requests from me. My friends often joke that it's almost as if I am driving the car and, if I try really hard, I can imagine that it is me behind the wheel.

Until recently, when I was at my home in London, I loved to ride the bus. I had to be accompanied but I was able to sit comfortably in my wheelchair in a London bus. We were never going anywhere special; I just wanted to see the city. We were just on the bus to nowhere and along for the ride. I liked the route that runs by all the fashionable designer shops in west London. I only dream about buying the clothes now but I still love to see what is happening in the world of fashion. Things have improved a lot for wheelchair users in the city these days but there is still a way to go before our society makes itself entirely open to those with disabilities. It's only when you have your own capabilities stripped from you that you realise just how crucial this is for a really inclusive society.

I came to realise just how precious these times were, when I had some freedom of movement, when I had an accident in my wheelchair in November 2023 on the steps at the entrance to my London home. This incident stripped me of all my confidence, and going outside has now become a source of great stress for me. Those trips on the bus or to a restaurant for lunch were some of the happiest moments of my long days and now I find myself panicking at the idea. When you are in such a vulnerable position it can be hard to bounce back from these things.

I have travelled whenever I could through the years. Regular trips to Tangier and an annual trip to a new destination became family traditions. Perhaps my illness has given these times added value in that I am profoundly grateful for each and every moment of them. For the last twenty-five years as the holiday season has approached, I have quietly acknowledged that this one might be the last one. For all these years, there has never really been a "next year" for me because that has never been a certainty. There

Now

has only ever been *this* year, *this* week, *this* day and *this* moment. A terminal diagnosis gives you a perspective on time that is quite unique. It isn't as much about "seizing the day" as valuing and treasuring the day and making good decisions about how you use your time. So every family holiday has been special and I am so grateful for those memories.

Some changes in my life have been for the better. Since my diagnosis, I have never been able to be certain how much time is left to me. The uncertainty has increased my appreciation of everything around me and all that I have. And it has also meant that I have built a clear view of what is really important in my life – what I know to be of real value. It's given me a sense of perspective on what really matters. It saddens me that there are so many people in this world who are ungrateful. They are never satisfied, cannot appreciate what they have and are always looking for more. They can never be in the moment and find joy there in the present. There are people who are jealous of others, or set out to hurt people in order to get what they think they want.

I also think enduring my own pain has meant that I have become very sensitive to others' needs. I cannot stand seeing anyone in pain because it reminds me of my own. My need to help them becomes almost wrapped up in my desire to relieve my own pain. I get a great deal of enjoyment out of helping others. I can't do much physically but I am blessed to have other ways of doing it. I am especially engaged when it comes to other MND sufferers. Some years ago, a young lady from the north of England came to my attention. She had been diagnosed with Motor Neurone Disease. And – like I was – she was a young mother. Perhaps, like me, she also felt her clock ticking because she wanted to take her daughter to Florida for the holiday of a lifetime. I saw myself in this woman, and was moved to help her. I made a donation to her funds so she could make her dream happen. Later, I contacted her and invited her and her family to Tangier. She came with her husband and her daughter. We had never met before but something bound us together immediately. The four of us had a lovely time together and she and I shared our experiences of living with MND. I think meeting up gave both of us tremendous strength and positive energy. We laughed a lot. Since then we have kept in touch regularly and I very much hope to see her again.

At a time when I was very depressed – worried about Mehdi's divorce and some issues my brother was navigating – I received a call from an old friend from London. Our story goes back over twenty years. At that time, my friend had been trying unsuccessfully for a baby for over ten years. I suggested adoption to her – there were many children in Tangier who were all alone. The problem was that she was not brave enough to ask her husband – she was worried about what he would feel about the prospect. I gladly told her I would speak to him, and I did. I managed to persuade him that this was a golden opportunity to be parents to a child who really needed them. I was happy when he agreed. Ahmed and I organised all the administrative requirements necessary for the adoption. I accompanied my friend on the visit to the orphanage in Tangier. There she adopted a three-month-old baby boy. A year later, she became pregnant with a baby girl. Her family was complete.

She had called me to invite me to the University of Cardiff. Her adopted son was graduating with a degree in medicine. I was elated to hear this. I was so happy. Helping others and making a difference in others' lives gives such great satisfaction and joy, especially when done without any expectation of receiving anything in return other than their happiness. This is my philosophy.

In recent years, I felt excited and energised by the viral Ice Bucket Challenge which increased funding for MND research and raised awareness about the condition. There seem to be many more MND diagnoses being made these days.

Now

This could be because we now understand more about the condition through the important research being done every year. But the process of diagnosis is also improving all the time. We understand more about this disease now, and I pray that there is a day when we can prevent or cure it. Throughout the years, I have never lost hope that this will happen. I have always kept myself up to date on treatments and trials taking place anywhere in the world.

My family have also never given up hope. They have contacted top specialists throughout the years, desperate to help me and to stop the progression of the disease. Sabrina went to New York and met with Dr. Hiroshi Mitsumoto, who is developing a new form of treatment which might help to delay the decline of patients with MND. I also have great confidence in the work being done by Professor Ammar Al-Chalabi at King's College, London.

In recent years, I have met with Dr. Georgios Kaltsakas, a breathing expert at St Thomas' Hospital. I was accompanied by Sabrina and Abdeslam. There were many other MND patients in the waiting room, some of them struggling for breath and many attached to a long tube through a hole inserted in the neck. Again, I was faced with the reality of what my future might hold and it was something I still found hard to accept. My brother noticed my distress and deliberately pushed my wheelchair into the hallway, pretending that he wanted to talk to me about something. Dr. Kaltsakas was terrific and, even though he was clearly busy, he made me feel that I was his only patient. If it was bad luck that brought me MND, it was good luck that brought me the many doctors who have looked after me. There are some amazing minds working on treatments for this disease and people like me.

When a person is diagnosed with MND, there is no hope, no surgery, no treatment or anything that can be done to stop it. And I do often contemplate how my life will end. My family have watched me lose my independence. I understand that dying is inevitable and that death is part of life. I pray for God's mercy and for my remaining time with my family to be peaceful until my time comes, and then I pray to Him for a gentle final exit from this life. The end scenario haunts me all the time. So many negative questions come to my mind. Will I choke, suffocate or slip into a coma and become motionless and mute – alive but also dead? Will I die at our home in London or, as I would prefer, in Tangier? Will I be like a prisoner attached to a variety of tubes and machines? No matter how strong and brave I try to be, I can never escape from these fears. I knew from the beginning, when I received my diagnosis in 1993, what this horrible disease would do to me and what the end might look like. When I think of it, I bite my lip and imagine the pain and frustration that my family will experience the day when I become only an observer and am not able to participate any more. I do not want my children to have a painful final memory of me. It is already so painful for my family to watch my body die, piece by piece. I have found myself in an internal turmoil about my final stages and how my beloved family will deal with this situation.

I recall watching a television programme some years ago. There was a woman with Multiple Sclerosis. She was advocating for her right to die. This shook me. To me, she looked relatively well. Yes, she was in a wheelchair, but her speech was clear and the movement of her arms and hands was normal. These were all things I had already lost to MND. The words from this poor woman made me sad because I began to compare my own situation to hers. I would have given anything to have the full use of my hands and arms back, and to be able to speak and make myself perfectly understood. If I had those things it would be easier to converse happily with my friends and family and I would be able to hug my grandchildren tight. I couldn't know if the woman had children or grandchildren but her rush to die upset me greatly.

Now

Because of my illness, I have often contemplated a person's right to die. Being a Muslim, I believe that all life is a sacred gift granted by Allah, and that is why I have fought so hard to cling to every moment of mine. But, having lived so much of my God-given life imprisoned in my failing body, the idea that my death should also be a kind of imprisonment is abominable to me. This raises the problem of a clash between my faith and the views of those who support the right to die. Intellectually, I can sympathise with the idea that anybody facing a terminal illness should have the right to choose their own exit. A death that is as dignified and pain-free, as far as is possible, is something we should wish for our fellow humans. When I think of my mother's passing, I think of how peaceful it was for her and for us, as a family. For myself, I would not ask for my passing to be accelerated, but neither would I want any artificial intervention to prolong suffering either for myself or for my loved ones. I think of Dylan Thomas's most famous poem where he urges us to not go "gentle" into the night and I find that I do not agree with that. On the contrary, I prefer the idea of slipping gently away from the confines of my earthly life.

However, the act of switching off life support for a loved one is something I wouldn't wish for anyone. I wish there was some way to protect my own children from the possibility that this will be their task, but there isn't. I also worry about what will come after I am gone. Family is so important to me. I sometimes feel that I am the glue that holds my family together. I worry that my disappearance will mean my family become distant from each other. I worry that, when I am gone, the relationships between my children will deteriorate or that there will be conflicts. My fears are perhaps exacerbated by the memories of things that happened between my mother and her siblings. After my grandfather's death, there was a bitter dispute between them over who would inherit his land. It caused a deep rift amongst his children – one that caused my mother great sadness. I hope that my children would never let anything like this come between them. I have raised my children to love, respect and care for each other and to stay united no matter what. My children have always had the example of myself and my brothers and of our close bond and support for each other. Of course, I cannot force the same relationship that I shared with my brothers on my children but it is my dearest hope that they remain united as a family unit and never *ever* turn their backs on one another.

No one – even me at times – thought that I would live to see my children grow up. But the impossible has happened. I am now a grandmother to four children. In order to navigate my family in the right direction, I have had to make many sacrifices and have faced endless challenges every single day. It feels like every day has been part of a struggle but it has been one worth fighting through. Somehow, it feels as though my sacrifices have been recognised by God and that I have been rewarded. And yet, I would be lying if I said that even my most wonderful moments have not been tinged with sadness.

I still love my life and I try to remain grateful for everything I have, every moment I am here and every piece of joy I find in being here. I am convinced that what has happened to me has been miraculous. All the doctors told me that I had only a couple of years to live. In that moment, I still remember how completely terrified I felt. And I had no way out. It felt like every door was closed in front of me. But what I did have was the power of the love I have for my family. And I also had the power of my faith in God and in my prayers. That was where I found my hope. That was where I found my strength.

I say that I miss being alone but, in many ways, I feel that I am always alone. I feel I am always alone with MND. It is me and the disease together, until whenever the end is. But my faith is there

Now

to remind me that I am not alone. It reminds me to acknowledge that there are others who are suffering more, and it reminds me to be grateful for the time I have and have had. Of course, I know that prayer and love for the family alone cannot cure any illness, but it certainly helps to give you the strength to keep going.

Although I might have been in denial about my illness during the years after my diagnosis, I always knew, in my heart, that responding with anger or frustration would lead nowhere good. It's natural to turn to feelings of anger when searching for a reason why something terrible has happened to you, but those feelings won't help you cope in any way. And I have always known that my time would be limited but I haven't allowed that to stop me thinking of the future and planning for it. That has been one of the ways I have kept my mind focused and engaged.

I don't want to be seen as brave or as a hero. That's not what I feel is true of me. What I want is to bring the lessons that living with MND has taught me to whoever is reading this book – which might be one of my own children or someone dealing with their own diagnosis or the diagnosis of a loved one. And what have I learned? I've learned that resilience comes through humour as much as from determination. I've learned to forgive and I've learned that if you let hatred and resentment rest in your heart they will corrupt everything. I've learned that denial will not see you through dark times and that you must instead find sources of strength to pull you back from those moments where you are at the brink. For me, the major source of strength has been my love for my family. For others, that strength might be loved ones, it might be faith or it might be simply that utterly human desire to cling to every moment of precious life that is yours. I've learned to be truly grateful for everything and every moment.

Afterword

Dear Abdeslam,

No one wants to say goodbye to someone they love, but it can be of great comfort to someone who is dying to be able to share their feelings.

My incredible brother, you are the beat of my heart, the soul in my body and you are my whole world. Without you, I would not have been able to survive all these years. Without you, my children would not be who they are now.

You have shown me what true love means. Your selflessness and generosity inspire me every day. I shall miss you so much, but I will always be looking over you and making sure that you are safe.

From the bottom of my heart, I thank you for your constant love and support.

Naima

To my beloved children,

This is the most difficult of letters to write – from dying mother to her children, after so many years of illness.

I have done everything that I could to stay alive as long as possible for you. You have been my reason for living. I want you to know that I am happy that each of you has developed your own individual character and attitude to life. I am incredibly proud of all of you for everything that you have already achieved and will go on to achieve in your lives. In the beginning, I did not want to share the reality of my illness with you, but I know now that we have shared this burden together. That knowledge has strengthened me in my life and I hope that it will always strengthen you in yours. As a family, our bond is so strong and I feel really blessed and grateful to Allah for this.

When I am gone, there are some things I would like you to remember. First, you must know that I will be watching over all of you *every* day of your lives. It is my dearest wish that the four of you stay united – no matter what happens or what the issue might be. Do not let anything drive you apart. Always try to resolve any disagreements between yourselves and do not let outside influences drive a wedge between you. Your paths might change and go in different directions as life goes on, but make sure that the bond of loyalty between you remains. My wish is that you stay united as a team – hand in hand, shoulder to shoulder – to overcome any obstacles and to defeat any enemy. Remember: "One for all and all for one." And remember that, as he is my special son, Mehdi is your special brother. Please continue to take care of each other as your uncle Ahmed wished and as I wish. Be good to each other, and to others. Always be mindful to help those in need of care and support. And always surround yourselves with good loyal people.

As you all know, Mummy is brave and is not afraid of dying. It is not that thought that causes me anguish, but the thought of leaving my brother, all of you and my grandchildren behind. I understand that my illness has caused each of you anxiety and sadness – taking away moments that should have been carefree and often casting a shadow over our days. Yet, despite the struggle and the suffering my illness has brought me, we have had such happy years together – and, though there have been tears, there has also been laughter. When my passing comes – yes, I know you will be sad, but I also want you to be happy in the knowledge that we have shared so much joy together. I want you to know that I am forever grateful for the love and care that you have shown me and for the little thoughtful touches that have so often cheered me on my way.

As my body has been so imprisoned, I have often had to use my memories to escape and I take those with me. You should know that I am forever happy with the treasured memories of picnics in the parks with my beloved children. Remember this. And build your own store of happy memories as the years go by.

Love you all so much.

Acknowledgements

First, my gratitude to all those who have shown kindness, support and understanding over the years; my family, my friends, my helpers and my doctors. Their support has enabled me to continue with my life.

Secondly, in relation to the production of the book, I would like to thank first my dearest Caroline Goldsmith for her invaluable editorial work. I would also like to thank Anna Baildon for her care in proofreading and Agnes Graves for her beautiful design work. I would also like to thank our dear friend Felipe Gonzalez for his foreword and of course my special friend Gerald Hattee for his introduction. Your words are much appreciated.

Thirdly, I would wish to acknowledge the constant love of my children, who have provided so much of my reason for living.